"*Memoirs of a Baby Stealer* is a compelling first-hand story of the true state of America's foster care system and why that system is in crisis. Though Mary Callahan writes of her experiences in one state, what happens in Maine is happening almost everywhere. This warm-hearted, but clear-headed account is essential reading for anyone who wants to know why things have gone so wrong in child welfare, and how to set them right."

—Richard Wexler, Executive Director,
National Coalition for Child Protection Reform

Memoirs
of a
Baby Stealer

Lessons I've Learned
as a Foster Mother

Mary Callahan

Pinewoods Press
Lisbon, Maine

Although the author and publisher have made every effort to ensure the accuracy and com-pleteness of information contained in this book, we assume no responsibility for errors, inaccuracies, omissions, or any inconsistency herein. Any slights of people, places, or organi-zations are unintentional.

First printing 2003

ISBN 0-9725983-0-8
LCCN 2002113520

ATTENTION CORPORATIONS, UNIVERSITIES, COLLEGES, AND PROFES-SIONAL ORGANIZATIONS: Quantity discounts are available on bulk purchases of this book for educational, gift purposes, or as premiums for increasing magazine subscriptions or renewals. Special books or book excerpts can also be created to fit specific needs. For informa-tion, please contact Pinewoods Press, PO Box 238, Lisbon, ME 04250; (207) 353-4223.

TABLE OF CONTENTS

✦ ✦ ✦

Prologue viii

Marie _____ 1

Chapter 1: The Spaghetti Rules 3

Chapter 2: At Least You Feed Me 8

Chapter 3: Archie and Edith 19

Chapter 4: Forgiveness and Small Hands 25

Chapter 5: Twenty-Seven Points 31

Chapter 6: You're Supposed to Cry 42

Tina _____ 51

Chapter 7: Rough Handling on the
Way to the Car 53

Chapter 8: Rough Handling in
the Parking Lot 62

Chapter 9: What Do You Think
"Partying" Means? 75

Brian _____ 81

Chapter 10: Syrup of Ipecac 83

Chapter 11: An Honest Mistake 93

Chapter 12: That Poor Child 99

Chapter 13: Good Days and Bad 105

Chapter 14: Foster Caretaking 113

Chapter 15: Negotiations 120

Chapter 16: Finding Jesse's Grave 125

Chapter 17: Hysterical and Over-involved 129

Amy Lynn —————————————————— 135

Chapter 18: Her Ideal Mother 137

Chapter 19: Fat, Dumb and Ugly 143

Chapter 20: Tryin' to Stop Lyin' 146

Chapter 21: Throwing in the Towel 154

Chapter 22: Retaliation 160

Chapter 23: A Story About Three Chickens 168

Stephen ————————————————————— 173

Chapter 24: "It Wasn't My Mom's Fault" 175

Chapter 25: Depressing the Counselor 181

Chapter 26: Price Tags and Broccoli 184

Chapter 27: Biting the Hand That Feeds 192

Mary ——————————————————————— 197

Chapter 28: Like Enron 199

Chapter 29: If I Ruled the World 204

Updates 207

Appendix 209

Additional Reading 224

Acknowledgments 225

To Heidi, Donna,
Bonnie, and Christine

PROLOGUE

✦ ✦ ✦

When I went into foster care I had no intention of writing about it, even though I had written about raising my own children in the book *Fighting for Tony*. People would often ask if I was writing a book and I would answer absolutely not. First, it is a violation of confidentiality and second, I didn't go into this to get writing material. I went into it to help kids.

By the time I started writing the book I had come to the conclusion that the only way to really help kids was to tell their stories. Though I wasn't sure if I had the nerve to go through with it. Maybe it was just a personal catharsis. So much had happened that I never believed possible, I felt I had to get it on paper, as much as anything, to get it out of my head.

That was early January of 2001. I was frustrated because a nine-year-old named Amy Lynn was living with me and DHS, meaning the Foster Care division of Department of Human Services, had cut off all contact with both of us.

Then, on January 31, I was watching the news and heard that a five-year-old girl named Logan Marr had been killed in her foster home. It was initially described as "an accident, an episode of discipline gone too far."

I immediately thought of Marie, my first foster child, who was abused badly in the foster home before mine, and of the excuses the social workers made for it.

As the days went by, more and more details came out about Logan's death. Foster mom, Sally Schofield, had put her in a high chair for time-out and it tipped over. No wait! Foster mom had duct taped her to the chair and it tipped over. No wait! Foster mom had duct taped her mouth and she suffocated and the chair tipped over.

Soon videotape was released to the media. It showed the child on her last visit with her birth mother, complaining about mistreatment by her foster mom. We hear a voice on the tape say, "Let's talk about happier things."

Again, I was reminded of Marie. Every time she tried to talk to social workers about the abuse she had suffered in a past foster home, they replied, "Let's just be happy you're in a better place now."

Then Logan's mother started to show up on the news. She was young, very sad, but surprisingly articulate. She blamed DHS for her daughter's death.

The DHS response: "Maybe if you had been a better mother in the first place, your daughter wouldn't have been in foster care and she wouldn't be dead."

What had that mother done? I asked myself. By then I knew how little it took to lose a child to the system. Could Logan's mother have done anything worse than was done to her in foster care? Worse than murder?

DHS tried to block that information from ever seeing the light of day. They invoked confidentiality rules every time they were asked, even as they hinted that it was pretty bad. At a training session I went to, the instructor said he knew people in DHS and we would all be shocked if we knew what he knew about Logan's mother.

I thought back on all the times I asked social workers how Marie could possibly have been better off with her abusive foster parents than with her own parents.

"Oh, you have no idea," they'd said. "Her parents are terrible people."

Just as I eventually learned that Marie's parents were nowhere near as terrible as her foster parents were, the state of Maine finally learned the truth behind the Marr case. The media got hold of the charges that had cost the grieving mother her child in the first place. It seems she: 1) moved too much, 2) allowed her daughter to witness her own abuse at the hands of a boyfriend, 3) let the child visit a grandfather who had been charged with sexual abuse of a minor (teenager) 20 years earlier, and 4) let the child get into "Jell-O shots" that were in the refrigerator at a party. It all adds up to neglect and failure to protect.

Yes, and Marie was taken from her family after an episode of discipline with a belt that was not too pretty either. But neither compared to what happened afterwards.

Every time a story came on the news adding a detail, I was enraged. How could a pattern like this exist yet no one seems to recognize it? No one seems to care?

I certainly learned that no one cared about Marie's story. I had been to higher ups at DHS about it. They seemed shocked at first, but quickly turned on me. I had been to the state legislature where I was told, "We have a hundred stories just like it. There is nothing new here."

When I heard that, as well as the fact the foster parents who speak to the state legislature usually end up getting their licenses yanked, I decided to move on, go back to raising the kids and forget it.

I planned on keeping my opinions to myself all the way through Marie, Tina and Brian. By Amy Lynn, I knew I had to at least get it on paper.

I'm ashamed to say the trigger for my change of heart was not what was being done to the child, but what was happening to me. I was defending myself against child abuse charges. Amy Lynn's DHS worker had filed charges against me, without telling me why or removing the child I was supposedly abusing. That was the last straw. After I finished documenting for my lawyer all that had happened with Amy Lynn, I went back to the beginning and started to write about Marie. I had just started when I heard the news about Logan Marr.

The Foster Care Crisis was front-page news. Reporters and editorialists demanded an investigation of the system that let Logan die. More details came out, like the fact that the DHS worker had not visited the child's foster home ever, in the four months the child had been there.

That was familiar to me from my experience with Amy Lynn. Her worker had never even met her until I called to complain.

DHS gave a public response to the revelation with regard to Logan Marr, claiming that they were doing a sweep of foster homes and weeding out the bad ones. My old friend Carol lost her foster kids when a surprise spot check uncovered plastic over one window and a smoke detector that didn't work. As if Carol's faulty smoke detector was some kind of indicator that some day she might duct tape a child to a chair and suffocate her.

Fortunately, the public wasn't buying it. The state legislature responded by setting up two committees to investigate the system, the Judicial Committee and the Health and Human Services Committee.

Prologue

A local TV program did a half hour on the problems at DHS. I emailed them afterwards with some of my thoughts and they immediately asked me if I would be willing to speak publicly.

I said no. The last thing I wanted was for my abuse complaint to be upgraded. I would hide my head in the sand, for one reason, and that was fear of retribution. Or should I say, further retribution.

I wondered how I would ever have the nerve to publish a book, if I didn't have the nerve to talk to a reporter on the record.

Then, some time in spring, the abuse complaint against me was resolved. I received an official letter telling me not to use Christmas as a bargaining chip anymore. I was being reprimanded for telling Amy Lynn if she didn't improve her behavior it would affect her Christmas haul. It was downgraded from abuse to a licensing violation and I was able to remain a foster parent, just not Amy Lynn's. Carol got a phone call asking her if she was ready to get back in the game. DHS begged for new foster parents in commercials on every TV and radio station. It was my voice in one of the radio commercials, something I did way back when I thought the system was helping kids and now regretted.

Then one day I was sitting at my computer, probably working on the book, when a thought elbowed it's way into my brain and completely took over. It was so compelling that I immediately went to my email and wrote it in a letter to myself. I've never opened it, because I know what it says. But every time I check my email it is there, one unread message, to remind me of what I realized that day. It goes something like this:

"God doesn't give you communication skills, and then expect you not to use them. There is a reason He has shown you all He has at a time in your life when you have very little to lose. You have no birth family in state to be targeted. You have a good career that can be used anywhere. And while you don't want to lose your foster care license and foster kids, if you do, you will fight even harder. The goal is to make sure these kids never lose their own kids to the foster care system, unless it is truly necessary."

Then I called back the TV reporter whom I had originally turned down.

Since then I have been on public TV, the local news and in the four major newspapers in the state. I have written editorials and letters to the editor. I have attended the committee meetings to investigate DHS and have given statements twice. I have emailed state legislators when I thought I had something to say that might enlighten them. On the anniversary of the death of that beautiful five-year-old girl, I participated in a press conference.

Oh, yes. There is another thing that popped into my head that day last spring. If I am going to go public, it has to be very public, so that it will make news if DHS retaliates against me. So far they have not.

I put the book aside from the time the committee meetings started in August until they ended in December. I wanted to give all my attention to the politics of it. When the committee meetings ended and their very weak response was made public, I got back to writing. I will deal with confidentiality issue by changing the names and identifying details. But I will keep trying to show people what I have seen and why it is so important to reform this system.

Bottom line: Too much power lies in the hands of individuals. DHS has become the new IRS, the schoolyard bully who will never be stopped because his daddy is a cop.

Marie

The little girls were well behaved. I might not have even known they were there, were it not for their tiny sneakers peaking out from under the curtain and the verbal abuse being hurled at them.

"Shut up, you little brats!"

"Sit down, you big babies!"

The woman is under a lot of stress, I told myself as I flew by taking care of other patients. I'm sure her husband is too. Being in an emergency room doesn't bring out the best in people. I wished I could detect a hint of feeling for the girls, something to indicate better parenting under the circumstances. There was none.

"Are you listening to that?" her nurse asked me when we ran into each other for a moment at the desk.

"Yeah," I answered. "I can't believe the way she talks to her children."

"Oh, those aren't her children," Donna told me. "Those are her foster kids."

CHAPTER 1

✦ ✦ ✦

The Spaghetti Rules

When people find out I am a foster parent, they often respond, "You must be a saint." If the child is there, they add something to the effect that he is lucky to have me. Nothing could be farther from the truth. They are not lucky. How could they be? They are in foster care and didn't choose to be.

I did choose to be a foster parent, though not because I am a saint or hope to be. I did it for many reasons, most of them cold and logical. Some of them were even mercenary.

For one thing I always wanted a big family. I came from a big family, having seven brothers and sisters before my parents started taking in foster kids of their own. But by the time I was having children it wasn't politically correct to add to the over population of the earth. Two kids was an acceptable number. Three was selfish and inconsiderate. Those who chose to have just one were the real saints.

I had two kids of my own with my husband Richard. To achieve my "big family," I wanted to adopt, but he wouldn't hear of it.

When we divorced after 14 years of marriage, I secretly believed I would find that person who loved a chaotic family life as much as I did; who thought the mantel should be cluttered with pictures of kids and grandkids. Instead I found men who were overwhelmed by the responsibility for their own children and looked forward, primarily, to getting theirs and mine out of the nest as soon as possible.

After one particularly bad break up, it dawned on me that I didn't need a man to raise children. I was already doing it without a man and enjoying it more. I called Agency A and the rest, as they say, is history. My standard response, when people ask me why I got into foster care, is:

"I decided to stop trying to raise grown men and go back to raising children. I'm better at that."

But there was more to it than that. My own children would be going off to college soon. I had a four-bedroom house that was worth less than I owed, thanks to my pattern of buying during a seller's market and selling during a buyer's market. The mortgage payment was a killer. I thought about getting a roommate, but to be honest, I didn't want someone who would be on an equal plane with me, who could legitimately complain about my housekeeping abilities. I didn't want to hear, "Would you please do something about that litter box?"

I wanted to say it. I wanted to say it to a kid! But kids are expensive and mine were about to get more expensive.

I could pay the bills if I worked two jobs and nurses can do that. I could work three 12-hour shifts at two different hospitals once the college tuition bills started coming in. Some people might find that more appealing than taking on more kids, but I didn't. I'll take kids any day.

Then there is the little matter of my hero complex. I understand it comes from being the older child of an alcoholic parent and growing up believing I could save the day if I tried hard enough. I never did save the day in my family of origin, but I did get some positive reinforcement for that behavior from my own kids.

My son, Tony, was diagnosed as autistic and retarded when he was two years old. By then I had a second child, Renee, as well. My first reaction to the news was sadness. I thought none of us would ever be happy again. Then my hero complex kicked in and I began to do research on autism. With that, and the hard work following the leads I got from the research, Tony's problems were eventually solved. It turned out his form of autism was actually caused by food allergy. By first grade there were no residual signs of the disorder.

I got a lot of positive feedback for that when the kids were young. (Publishing *Fighting for Tony* didn't hurt!) But now I had two surly teenagers and looked back with fondness on the earlier challenges. Those were the good old days. I wanted to do that again…and be able to pay the bills doing it. That would be the ideal situation.

Kids with problems (read between the lines, who would appreciate me), no men, and bills paid. It all added up to foster care.

But I didn't really feel up to chasing toddlers again. I had my own kids when I was almost thirty, so the aches and pains of middle age were kicking in. I needed my sleep, so babies were out. The kids that appealed to me were the ones you saw back then on talk shows, the kids deemed "unadoptable" because of their age. Every time Phil or Oprah did a show like that I wrote down the phone number on the screen at the end of the show.

Those were the kids I wanted. I didn't want to see my name in the paper on Mother's Day because I had fostered 312 kids in 25 years. I definitely didn't want to be known for quantity.

I didn't even want to be known for quality. I have no illusions that I am the best mother on the planet. I wanted to be known for security. I wanted kids to say they finally had a home, that they could be kids again, because they didn't have to worry about where they would be going next.

It all added up- the big family fantasy, the financial problems, the hero complex. It all added up to long-term foster care.

I met Marie at the Agency A Christmas party on my 45th birthday. She was a skinny little 12-year-old with that sharp cheek- boned, straight nose kind of beauty seen in fashion models, sadly hidden under a mop of straw-like blond hair. But she was angry, refusing to make eye contact with at me. I didn't expect her to be unhappy that she had to spend the weekend with me, but she was going to miss her foster mother's 35th birthday party.

"You're kidding!?" I exclaimed. "It's my birthday too."

Marie's life was full of coincidences. Her foster parents had the same first names as her birth parents, Donald and Cheryl. Her foster parents and her DHS worker had almost the same last names, Reedy and Reed. Now her new respite foster mother was 10 years to the day older than her regular foster mother. It was enough to peak her interest.

"Come on," I coaxed her, "We'll have our own party. We'll go out for pizza." She left without looking back.

Marie and I just clicked. We went to Pizzeria Uno and I let her drink coffee. We talked about boys. We talked about music. We talked about clothes. We even talked about sex. She had a lot of questions and as a nurse educator, I had a lot of answers. When she wore out that subject, I told her what to expect from Tony and Renee who were working and playing hard that weekend, but would be around more in the future. We talked about my family, but we didn't talk about hers, either birth or foster. It was the elephant in the living room.

We both knew she was with me because her foster mother needed a break from her. I'd been told Marie had become mouthy, was using bad language, and disobeying her foster parents. I had that side of the story. I got a hint of the other side during a spaghetti dinner. But I didn't recognize it as a hint until later when I looked back on it from a more knowing vantage point.

Marie apologized when she couldn't get her spaghetti noodles to wrap perfectly around her fork. A look of stark terror crossed her face when the next bite didn't go any better.

"Don't worry about it," I said.

"Really?" she asked, blue eyes wide. "I don't mean to break any rules."

"You mean the spaghetti rules?" I joked.

"Yeah," she answered in all seriousness.

"We don't have spaghetti rules."

She laughed, but tentatively, still waiting for me to clarify.

"Honestly, " I said, "We're not neat freaks around here." She finally stopped waiting for more and went back to eating. The rest of the meal was uneventful. Later I would learn that she had lived six years in a household where imperfect manners, even spaghetti hanging from the fork, meant leaving the table without finishing the meal. Chewing too fast or too slow could end a meal. Having a piece of food fall from the fork meant going to bed hungry. Even leaning back against the chair back was an infraction that left no room for second chances.

I didn't see any disruptive behavior from Marie. I just saw a delightful, if a little bit timid, angel. I enjoyed her so much I was sorry to have to take her back home on Sunday. The plan was that she would spend one weekend a month with me and that seemed an awfully long stretch. I wanted to give her a token of my affection, so I scoured the Sunday paper for Christmas crafts fairs we could hit on the drive back. I found one at the Steep Falls Baptist Church.

We poked around there and I waited for her to express interest in some knickknack or Christmas ornament. But she was strangely quiet except to agree with me on everything.

"Oh, isn't that pretty!"

"Yep."

"Look at that darling snowman!"

"Uh huh."

Finally I just had to spill it. "I wanted to get you a little Christmas present while we are here. Isn't there anything you like?"

"I did see a bracelet…" I spent $17 on the bracelet. It was just a rope of purple stones strung together on a wire, but she seemed delighted, so I was too.

The feedback I got via the social worker was that Donald and Cheryl were unhappy. They hadn't expected Marie to be rewarded for all the trouble she had caused at their home. They took the bracelet and Marie never saw it again. I didn't see Marie again for 5 months.

CHAPTER 2

✦ ✦ ✦

At Least You Feed Me

By May I was pretty depressed about the foster care business. I had taken in another 12-year-old girl named Nicole, for six weeks of pure hell. Every day was a new kind of disaster. She ran away. She took an overdose of pills. She stabbed a stranger at the movie theater. She called her lawyer and said I was a drunk. I later learned she was trying to get thrown out in hopes of being returned to her grandmother. When I told her the arrangement wasn't working out for me, she made sure I wouldn't change my mind by trashing my house. The police had to be called to stop her. There was a used Kotex under my pillow when I went to bed that night. I was so exhausted, I didn't notice it until morning.

There were a couple more weekend kids, but none of them touched my heart like Marie. Then one afternoon my daughter Renee and I were in adjoining changing rooms at Goodwill when she called through the thin wall.

"I forgot to tell you. There was a message on the answering machine. Marie needs a permanent placement. They want to know if you're interested. Do you believe it?"

She must have expected a quicker response from me.

"Oh, my God, you're considering it!" she shouted, after a pause. "Didn't you learn anything from Nicole?"

"Marie is not Nicole."

8

If I was depressed, Renee and Tony were totally burned on the foster care idea. To be honest, they never were enthused but merely supported it because I pointed out that they owed me that much. They hadn't spent much time with Marie on her first and only visit. But they had spent plenty of time with Nicole. They practically threatened a walkout if I took in another child, but I made a deal with them. I told them to decide after one more weekend with Marie, this time actually hanging out together.

A month later, Marie was their cherished new little sister and I had some of that big family chaos I always wanted. Renee and Marie were running back and forth between bedrooms trading clothes and jewelry every morning. Tony's baseball cap was forever being held hostage by one of the girls. Except for the fact that Marie was short and blond, while my birth-kids were tall and dark, you would have thought they had all grown up together.

The social workers thought the transition would be hard on Marie. They said her problems with Cheryl occurred because they were too much alike and that Marie would have to grieve the loss of that relationship. That was not my impression. To me, the hard part was that we could not get away from Cheryl fast enough. For six weeks I took Marie for the weekend and then brought her back home so she could finish sixth grade in the same school she started in. Both Marie and Cheryl took every opportunity to tell me horror stories about the other. I tried to appear neutral, not to say anything to either that could make me seem controversial if quoted later to the social workers. I didn't want anyone questioning whether my home was a suitable placement for Marie.

But there was one time when I could not keep my mouth shut. It was about Marie's sixth grade graduation.

The plan was that the Reedys would bring her to the ceremony, both families would attend, and then Marie would go home with us. Marie wanted to wear a little denim dress I had given her for her 13th birthday and a new pair of chunky black shoes. Cheryl and Donald protested, as I learned via a phone call from an Agency A social worker.

"Their feeling is that it's not fair to the other kids in the family. She's the one that has caused all the problems and yet she gets a new dress and shoes. They want her to wear something she already has, like a pair of pants and a sweater."

That was the last straw. "Wasn't throwing her out enough?" I asked. "Does she also need to be humiliated in front of her classmates? You know I would think, when it comes to consequences of bad behavior, some things would be sacred. It's her graduation! If they can't see that and you can't see that, maybe she should just move in with me a day early!"

She wore the denim dress, and the subject never came up again. I don't know who was happier to see the Reedy's house and the town of Waterboro become distant in the rearview mirror, Marie or me. We had only one contact with them that summer when we ran into them at an outdoor festival. The next day I got a call from the social worker.

"Cheryl said she ran into Marie over the weekend and she looked like a slut."

"I was there. She was in a T-shirt and overalls, nothing tight, nothing see-through. She had on mascara."

"I figured as much. I had to call. Sorry."

Every time I told social workers how well things were going that summer, they reminded me that it was "the honeymoon phase." I knew they were right. But I figured it was nice having that time, that we were building a foundation to get us through the inevitable post honeymoon phase. I was wrong about that. Later I would realize that getting through the good times is no test of a relationship. Anyone can do that. It's the bad times that really cement things. It's having loving feelings again after thinking you never would that creates a bond between people. That was coming.

The honeymoon came to a screeching halt when the summer did. After weeks of going to the beach to check out the boys, a first airplane flight and a vacation to New Mexico, real life kicked in. I expected it to be a bumpy ride. Marie had never been a good student. She barely scraped by sixth grade and was starting seventh in the lowest level class with an hour a day of special help.

"I'm not going to see that woman, that Mrs. Flewelling!" she told me.

"Why not?"

"She's stupid."

"Can you get good grades without her help?"

"I don't give a care."

10

Actual schoolwork was the least of her problems. Behavior issues caused my phone to ring all day. She talked back in class. She refused to leave art, the only class she liked, and move on to the next subject. She threatened a grade school child on her way home from school. She called a teacher a fucking asshole (though in her defense, at the meeting I had to attend on that one, I learned she was right). There was no discussing any of it at home. She just turned and walked away when I tried. I was working full-time as an office nurse and worried that I would soon be taking vacation time if she got suspended.

She wasn't much fun at home either. She spent all her time lying on the couch, watching television and eating, and eating, and eating. She packed on 25 pounds before my eyes. The new school clothes I'd bought her at Club 21 were either bulging at the seams or not wearable at all. My grocery bill doubled. I didn't know what to say. I didn't want to be responsible for triggering anorexia. I didn't get on Tony and Renee about snacking, but then they were both thin as rails.

I hated myself for the fact that the weight bothered me as much as it did. They told us in foster parenting class that we would learn more about ourselves in this business and I was learning that I was shallow. I didn't expect that. But here was the proof. I only loved her when she was cute, like some kind of trophy kid. This was not working out.

The theory is that these kids come with a support team, usually a therapist they see weekly and a social worker or two assigned to the case. These are the people you call when you need to strategize or just to vent. Marie came without a therapist. She had flat out refused to see one in the past and when forced, sat silently for the entire hour. But her social workers were among the best I would ever deal with.

You may wonder why I rarely mention the social workers by name and the answer is simple. The names change all the time. The turnover in the business is astonishing. By the time Marie was out of her honeymoon phase, we were on our second social worker. But the caliber of social worker was high at Agency A. They were there when I needed them and they were intuitive.

I think it was Jean who made me realize that I had given up too much. With all the issues I had to deal with, the one that really kept me gritting my teeth was one that sounds minor by comparison. It was the TV. It wasn't mine anymore and neither was the couch in front of it. Marie never sat on the couch. She reclined. I had to ask her to move her feet every time I sat down, then she kept them wedged against my thigh as if I was the one in her way. She crunched Doritos when she wasn't cracking her knuckles and every other joint in her body. Between crunching and cracking, she asked questions.

"Why doesn't that Kramer guy have a job?"

"I don't know."

"Well that's stupid. None of them have jobs. Is Elaine married to Jerry?"

"No."

"Are they married in real life?"

"Marie, I'm trying to watch."

"Okay." Crunch, crunch, crunch. "Why would anyone go out with George? He's ugly."

I had also lost my quiet Sunday mornings with the newspaper and a cup of tea. It was my habit to make a big breakfast on Sundays, but not until I was done with the paper. That drove Marie crazy. She nagged and nagged and when that didn't work she asked me to explain every headline or looked at the comics and complained they weren't funny.

She had stolen my downtime. She had taken those few things that were just for me. And I let her. She was in charge now and I was flapping in the breeze wanting to strike back at her, but restrained by the guilt I felt. The solution was simple.

I turned an upstairs bedroom into a second TV room just for kids! And I never even had to say why. I did institute a new rule, that she could only come downstairs for breakfast on Sunday when I called her, after my tea. She didn't mind anymore, since she had the TV. And with that I was back on my throne, thanks to Jean.

Once I got my bearings again, I was ready and willing to work on Marie's problems. That lesson has stayed with me. It sounds so trite, but it is true. You have to put yourself first in a few key areas or you can't be effective with kids. Now I may be the only foster parent for whom the key areas are inane sitcoms and Parade Magazine, sadly confirming my last self-discovery that I am shallow, but there it is.

I was grateful for my kids, Tony and Renee, during that first year with Marie. While my own relationship with her deteriorated, the problems at school had absolutely no effect on her relationship with them. They still thought she was the best and cutest little sister in the world. She and Renee still talked about clothes and boys, shopping in the Old

Port during those rare moments when Marie wasn't grounded. Tony had a teasing (but only about safe stuff) kind of relationship with her, much like the one he had with Renee. I wouldn't be the least bit surprised if the two of them were also willing sounding boards when she complained about me, but that's okay. I didn't want her to feel alone. I hoped she still thought this was a good place to live and apologized to her once for being on her case again.

"I feel bad that I have to ground you all the time. I don't want to turn into another Cheryl…" at which point she began waving her arms to stop me from continuing.

"At least you feed me!" she exclaimed.

Then she launched into a tirade about eating at the Reedy's. That's when I learned that she was sent from the table at the slightest infraction of the rules, rules as ridiculous as "Sandwiches are to be eaten with one hand not two." She told me that Cheryl sat across from her at the dinner table to count how many times she chewed a minute so she could be punished if she was too fast or too slow. She told me that, while she rarely finished a meal, she was brought back out of her room after a meal to clean up after everyone else. The Reedys had four children of their own, as well as Marie's sister Linda, but none of them had to live by the same rules and none of them ever had to do the dishes.

Marie also told me that Cheryl had a special cabinet of food for the foster children, all generic or cheaper brands of food than she had for her own family. Foster kids got cold cereal for breakfast while the Reedy kids ate French toast or eggs and bacon. Foster kids were offered only water with meals. Sometimes they were offered an alternative, half a glass of Kool-aid.

The more I heard the angrier I got and I frequently made a special phone call to the social worker to relay one of Marie's stories.

"Do you realize they were withholding food as punishment?" I asked after that conversation.

"They were pretty much out of ideas of things to withhold from Marie. That was a last resort."

"You approved of that? You mean if I decided to just feed two meals a day, or keep a separate cabinet of cheap food just for Marie, that would be okay with you?"

"No, that wouldn't be okay with me," she almost hissed into the phone. "Why do you think I got her out of there? From the minute I got this case I've been trying to get her out of there. But my bosses wouldn't hear of it."

"Why? What's in it for them to put Marie through that?"

"Nothing. They just didn't think it had gone over the line yet, and they didn't want to put Marie through the trauma of a move."

"And Agency A's claim to fame is that 75% of their placements last! And Marie would skew their statistics. Was that it?"

"I don't think that played a role. You know Cheryl was the best thing that ever happened to Marie in the beginning. She probably saved her life."

"How?"

"She's alive, isn't she? She was suicidal when she got there."

I had no argument for that, but Marie did.

"I was never suicidal," she shouted, when I brought the subject up later. "They keep saying I jumped out of a moving car. That car was barely moving. I was trying to run away. I hated my first foster parents, the Otts. Their son was mean to me and he came into my room at night and showed me his thing. I just wanted to go home."

I got such different versions of the past from Marie than I got from the social workers. Marie often used her old friends from Waterboro to verify her stories. They backed her up, but to me the fact that she had old friends from Waterboro was verification enough. Cheryl had told me when I picked her up for the weekend once, that Marie had no friends.

"In six years, no one has ever called to talk to her. She was never invited to a birthday party. No one likes her."

I was at a loss for words and Marie was actively shoving me out the door towards the car. I didn't correct her rude behavior because I didn't want to continue the conversation anyway. When we got in the car she was slouched in the seat and pouted for a few minutes and then announced that she had not only been invited to birthday parties, she even went to one.

Once she moved in with us, the phone never quit ringing for Marie. I drove back and forth to Waterboro almost every weekend to pick up friends or drop Marie off. Once, when Jenny was spending the night, I waited until Marie was in the shower to ask the question that had been on my mind.

14

"Why didn't you girls get together with Marie when she lived close by? Cheryl said you never called to invite her over."

"Are you kidding?" she gasped. "We were scared to death of Cheryl. And we did call. Cheryl would say Marie was busy or she wasn't home. She was such a bitch, excuse my French. Once I was trading some food with Marie at lunch in the school cafeteria and Cheryl walked in and took the candy bar right out of Marie's mouth."

"What was she doing at school?"

"Oh she was always there, hanging around, spying on Marie."

Marie later told me that Cheryl was there because she volunteered in her son Justin's classroom. But she added that Cheryl had told her that night that if she ever saw Marie eating anyone else's food again, she would bring a high chair to school and put a bib on her and feed her by hand.

It was hard to leave the past in the past as the social workers encouraged. But they always had the last word, the ace in the hole.

"Marie's sister Linda denies everything she says. I've asked her myself. She says Marie is lying. Marie does have a history of lying."

"And Jenny is lying?"

"Apparently."

"Linda is the one who has reason to lie. She's the golden child in that house. Why would she mess that up?"

"I've promised not to get her in trouble."

"She's smarter than that. She watched what happened to Marie after you people promised to protect her. She got punished as soon as you left. Linda would be crazy to complain about Reedys while she's still living with them."

"Maybe."

"If Marie is telling the truth and Linda is lying to save her own skin, then she's going through her own kind of hell in that house,"

"I've thought of that. But Linda denies it."

To tell the truth, we had enough problems in the present to keep us from dwelling on the past. Since most of the problems were confined to school, I was looking forward to a break from them over Christmas vacation. I got that and more. I got a light bulb moment that would change the course of Marie's life. That was my Christmas present.

I love to Christmas shop, especially for girls. Like Renee, Marie wanted clothes and jewelry, jewelry and clothes. Marie was looking a little better in her clothes too, having stretched out a few inches without putting on any more weight. She had the beginnings of a womanly body, unlike the year before when she was straight up and down. Plus, her blond hair was shiny and healthy looking now, cut to just below her chin. I always enjoyed dressing my kids up. From the time Renee and Tony were little, I was accused of treating them like favorite dolls. Tony eventually complained. The girls never did.

Another gift I liked to give, also a little self-serving, was a show in Boston. I got Renee tickets to see *Rent* with her dear, sweet, old mother. And Marie reached into her stocking and pulled out tickets to *Grease*.

Tony said he would rather jump off a bridge than sit through a musical, so I went another direction with him. Renee was thrilled with her present. Marie said thanks, but didn't seem to know what to make of it.

Grease was showing just a few days after Christmas. I was pulling a few shifts at a local hospital to pay for Christmas and happened to be at work the evening before we were going to Boston. It was slow and I decided to spend some time planning the trip. I called Marie from work to get some information.

"Marie, do you remember the name of the theater where GREASE is showing?"

"No."

"Could you get out the tickets and look?"

"I don't know where they are."

"On the first shelf in the kitchen."

"I'm kinda busy now."

"Marie!"

She retrieved the tickets.

"It doesn't say what theater."

"Of course it does."

"No, it doesn't!"

"Well, what does it say?"

"Just *Grease* and the date."

"Oh, for heaven sakes, Marie! Read me the whole ticket. Starting in the upper left corner."

She let out an exasperated sigh. "Okay. It says C-O-L-O-N-I-A-L-T-H-E-A..."

"Wait a minute. That says Colonial Theater. I thought you said it didn't say the theater?" "Look, I was in the middle of a TV show."

"Well, don't let me put you out any," I said sarcastically. "I'm only taking you to Boston."

She was silent.

"What time is the show tomorrow?" I asked finally.

"It doesn't…oh here it is. Three o'clock."

After hanging up I turned to my co-workers to complain about the ingratitude of teenagers, but the light was beginning to dawn. When I got home that night, the *Grease* tickets were sitting on the kitchen table. Not only was Colonial Theater in big bold letters, but the show was a two o'clock, not three.

Marie couldn't read.

Things got worse before they got better, kind of like the storm before the calm, but at least I understood why. Marie had spent so many years, and so much energy, trying to conceal and distract from her perceived inadequacy. Now she was busted. The testing I arranged for and dragged her to against her will indicated many huge gaps in her learning, but no lack of intelligence.

While she had always attended school, her education was disrupted frequently by moves before and after going into foster care. I can only imagine how much school time she spent staring at the blackboard and worrying about what horror she would be confronted with when she got home. How could she be expected to concentrate on or even care about such minor issues as reading and math?

Now I understood why she thought the state she lived in was Portland and the town was Maine. And I knew why, when I gave her a ten dollar bill and sent her to the cash register to pay for a pair of earrings at Claire's, she always changed her mind about getting them. She would have no idea if she got the right change back. Now I knew why she kept herself in the center of controversy at school. It was less humiliating to be the tough kid than the dumb kid.

Once the testing was done, tutoring began. A little school in South Portland called The Learning Achievement Center gave her back her self-esteem. I tried working with her myself at first. We sat across the kitchen table from each other with a pile of coins and ran through different shopping scenarios, something we could both get into.

"Okay, I'm buying these earrings for $6.25. I give you a ten. Give me my change."

It would go well for a few minutes and then she would get something wrong and become defensive. She was always sure I was wrong and she was right. She was gone from the table before I could explain why the change would be $3.75, and not $4.75. I decided it would be better for both of us if she went to tutoring elsewhere. I insisted on professional tutors at the LAC, not a local high school kid, and had to write a letter to Agency A to get them to agree to pay for it. They did, and I drove her two evenings a week. On the advice of the director of the school, I also got her a Franklin Speller, a little, calculator-sized device that she could punch letters into and be told what they spelled. She started reading simple books, but didn't have to be embarrassed by them because she could work in the privacy of her bedroom and ask the tiny computer when she needed help. That summer she went to a special camp called *Super Camp*, recommended by The Learning Achievement Center. That continued her catch-up education.

And thus we come to another lesson in foster parenting. Find the gems in the community and use them. There are people out there, tutors, karate teachers, etc. who work with kids and do their jobs very well. Step back and let them. Another spin on that might be that I discovered I'm not only shallow, but also lazy. I think I'll go with the first spin.

CHAPTER 3

✦ ✦ ✦

Archie and Edith

Marie started her last year of middle school quietly and calmly. She no longer had anything to fear. She had learned enough in tutoring to hold her own in any classroom situation. When I attended her first parent/teacher conference, the word that kept coming up was "delightful." One of the teachers had been her teacher the year before as well, so he understood why I chuckled each time I heard the word again. He agreed it was hard to believe she was the same child.

Marie wasn't the troublemaker at school and she wasn't the blob on the couch at home anymore either. She was too pretty not to have a busy social life. She looked like a California girl by now, flowing blond hair and blue eyes that sparkled even without all that glitter she loved so much. She auditioned for and was accepted into modeling classes. I knew everyone whose parent would pay got accepted, but Marie didn't know that so it was quite an ego boost. Later that school year she took private voice lessons and was able to perform at the school talent show. She sang Truly, Madly, Deeply, (a popular ballad by Savage Garden) so well that some people thought she was lip-synching.

There was relative peace on the home front. Marie and I had the house to ourselves now. Renee was at Tulane in New Orleans. Tony was at a broadcasting college in Bangor. I don't know how Marie felt, but I was glad to see them go.

I never thought I would say that. Renee and I had been so close when she was younger. We joked that we would have to start fighting some day or we would never be able to separate. I would have been all right with that, in theory, knowing that once she established herself as an independent person, we would renew our bond. I just didn't think the things we would be fighting about would be drugs, alcohol and boyfriends with criminal pasts.

I worried about Marie's exposure to all this, but I also felt it was no different than what might have gone on in any home. She was witnessing family problems, but hopefully handled right or right enough. Teens and drugs are a difficult issue. There is not the agreement among adults one might expect. Many parents believe it is a right of passage and turn their heads to a certain amount of drug use. I had a lot of people reassuring me that Renee was just "experimenting," like we all did. But I didn't. I was a straight arrow as a teenager. My friends and siblings weren't and some are dead now because of it. I found I couldn't turn my head and I finally came to the conclusion that it wasn't up to anyone but me to decide what my limits were. I took a very hard line stance, basically zero tolerance.

At one point Renee moved out and spent a month living with the boyfriend with a criminal past and his friends. She learned some hard lessons before moving home and getting into substance abuse counseling. When she got on the plane for New Orleans, I was relieved to see her go. I think Tony and Marie were just relieved not to be caught in the middle of our feuding any more. If nothing else, Marie had a preview of what would go on if she chose to follow Renee's path.

So Marie became my only child fifteen months after moving in with me. And I was her only parent as she was still estranged from both of her birth parents. This cozy little arrangement wouldn't last.

Now that Marie could read, she no longer hated school and all teachers. She became quite outgoing in class and even stayed after class to talk. She kept her past no secret. Everyone knew she was in foster care, lucky for me since she once announced in English class that her mother was a whore and everyone knew she didn't mean me. She told me about it later because the teacher kept her after class to discuss it.

I asked her, "What do you mean by whore?"

"A really bad person," she answered.

"It means a little more than that," I said. "It usually means a woman who has sex with a lot of different partners, sometimes for money."

She shrugged. "That's just what Cheryl always said."

"I wouldn't go by that," I told her, but I wasn't the only one planting the seed of doubt. Her teacher, after hearing why she made that shocking statement about her mother, spoke to her on the subject of forgiveness.

By then I had had some contact with Marie's birth parents, meeting each of them once at DHS. Her father was grumpy and her mother ditzy. They reminded me of a poorer and more modern day version of Archie and Edith Bunker. They didn't seem like bad people, but I knew they were bad enough parents to have lost custody of their daughters, so I didn't have much respect for them.

They were divorced and both had supervised visits originally, but Marie had refused to see her mother since she was nine. She still saw her dad once a month when she first moved in with me, but did so like it was an unpleasant duty. Even those visits stopped when he had the nerve (in her eyes) to go back to court to try to regain custody of Marie and Linda shortly after Marie moved in with me.

She was terrified that he would succeed and wrote a scathing letter to the judge in order to prevent it. I proofread the letter for her, knowing the grammar and spelling would be atrocious, but not expecting to be so disturbed by the content. It was pure hate.

"You know, Marie," I said. "I think I would say less about how much you hate him and more about why. Those strong feelings have to come from somewhere. Be specific. Tell a story or two."

She wrote it again, but changed it very little. The only story she told was the one I already knew and it was many years old.

Before I even met Marie I had read her file and learned of the incident that brought her into state custody. It seems Marie, Linda and their older brothers, Randy and Matt, were living with their father after the divorce. He had a girlfriend named Pam who was also living with them and Pam had a cat. One day the cat turned up with it's tail shaved. Pam was livid.

When dad got home from work, he wanted to know who did it and no one confessed. His solution was to beat it out of them and since he didn't know who to beat, he sat them around in a circle, set a timer, and asked again every time it went off, who shaved the cat. If no one admitted it, they all got hit with a belt. Pam, in frustration that this was getting them nowhere, made a secret phone call to a friend who was a security guard. She came to the door in uniform and pretended she was a cop about to arrest all of them if none of them talked. Even that didn't work. The beatings, or spankings depending on who's telling the story, went on late into the night. Marie finally said she had shaved the cat. All the other kids were told to hit her as much as they had been hit to pay her back for keeping quiet so long.

Apparently a lot of noise came out of the apartment that night because a neighbor called the real police in the morning. The four kids were taken from their classrooms and examined by doctors the next day. They were asked how they got the bruises and welts. All but Marie told stories of falling down stairs or off bicycles. Marie was too young to think of covering for her father. She told the truth.

As it turned out, it was the first time she told the truth about the incident. It seems she was lying the night before when she said she had shaved the cat. Courageously, she took the blame to get it over with for all of them. It was later learned that her uncle Bob did it while drunk the night before. One irony that would come out of this whole saga is that telling the truth got Marie taken from her family and blamed by them for all the years in foster care. Telling the lie got her file stamped "History of Lying" so that she was never believed again.

Marie brought that incident up in the letter and it was the first time I had the flickering thought, "Is that all there is?" Sure it was nasty. But no bones were broken and no one needed stitches. I am a nurse. I've seen plenty of child abuse. I was sure there was more than this. Once, when I was complaining to the social workers about the Reedys, I asked if the girls wouldn't have been better off with their real parents and the worker shook her head and said, "You have no idea." I took that to mean there were details they couldn't tell me, but I would be shocked if I knew.

I was called to testify in court, mostly about Marie's present living situation, and to introduce the letter into evidence. I was so relieved that I didn't have to read it out loud. It was embarrassingly venomous and at least as much of it was directed at Cheryl Reedy as was directed at Marie's dad. And Cheryl was sitting in the back row. That was a can of worms I didn't want to open in that setting.

The judge ruled in DHS's favor and the girls stayed in state custody, but I walked out with an unsettled feeling. Marie's dad didn't seem like such a bad guy. When I heard his side, particularly the lengths he had gone to get the girls back, I hurt for him. He had taken every class DHS asked him to take, particularly the anger management and parenting classes. And this wasn't the first time he had spent hard-earned money on a lawyer only to hear the story of the cat's tail, the timer and the security guard trotted out again and costing him his kids. Unfortunately he couldn't afford much of a lawyer. The guy I saw looked like he'd slept in his over-sized black suit and I wasn't sure he was sober. As we walked out of court, our social worker leaned over to me and whispered conspiratorially, "With a better lawyer, he would have won."

Donald cornered me in the parking lot, and for a minute I thought I was about to witness his dark side first hand. But it wasn't that. He just wanted to explain himself to me so I could relay it to Marie. He seemed desperate and sad, but not dangerous. He said he was sorry for what he had put her through by going back to court. But he felt that, if she was going to be moved from Reedy's, she should be moved back home. After all, the boys were with him and they were fine. But Marie and her sister kept insisting they were happy where they were and then suddenly it turns out Marie wasn't so happy after all.

"Why can't she come home," he asked me. "And why does she hate me so much. Everybody makes mistakes." I couldn't answer that.

Marie and her dad only saw each other one more time after that day in court. She was snotty. He was defensive. Neither requested another visit after that.

The time I met Marie's mother in the DHS parking lot was much the same. She was a little harder to talk to, words flying out of her mouth like machine gun rounds, subjects changing like right angles on a roller coaster. It was work standing out in the cold listening to her, trying to follow her train of thought. But in the middle of it, she made some good points too. She wasn't even there when the abuse happened. She was living in another state. She came back as soon as she heard, but DHS had to investigate her fitness before the kids could live with her again. They decided she was unstable, in her telling, just because she'd been married three times.

"Whoa!" I got interested there. "I've been married three times."

For just a moment we were sisters-in-arms, commiserating about our bad luck with men. Funny that she lost her children over it...and I got to keep one of them in spite of it.

After our day in court, I went straight to Marie's school to tell her that we had won. She hugged me and cried in the hallway. Then, in typical Marie fashion, she pointed out that my roots were showing. I thought about how much her speech pattern was like her mother's. And her eyes were like her dad's.

I felt like a baby stealer, but I didn't want to give her back. She was my daughter now, wasn't she? We had been through the rough times, and come out the other end a family, right? Love has to count for something. Sleep was hard to come by for a while with so many questions on my mind and so much guilt to assuage.

CHAPTER 4

✦ ✦ ✦

Forgiveness and Small Hands

Marie surprised everyone when she announced that she wanted to see her mother again. So far in life she had demonstrated such a strong will. When she said she was never speaking to someone again, even a whole category like counselors, she meant it. But a mother is a different story. She held out 5 years in her vow never to speak to her mother again, but an interested English teacher said the right words and allowed Marie to save face and change her mind at the same time. The teacher spoke of forgiveness, and Marie decided to forgive her mother.

By this time, we were assigned to a social worker named Susan who made all the arrangements. Susan got to give mom the good news, then set about to plan the reunion in great detail. It was decided they would meet in a family room at Agency A. The room was booked for an hour and Susan and I would stay with Marie unless she signaled that it was okay for us to go. Mom was coached on appropriate topics of conversation and encouraged to really listen to Marie, not just to talk, and also to avoid rehashing the past too much. A few days before the meeting, Susan came out to the house to do some advance work with Marie.

We sat in the upstairs TV room and I listened while Susan painstakingly outlined the plan to Marie. I found myself cringing at her patronizing tone. I knew she meant well, but she was trying to control this event as if the outcome was life or death. I was afraid it was being blown so big that Marie might back out. Instead, she exploded.

"I am not a science experiment!" she announced suddenly jumping off the couch she shared with Susan. "She's my mother and I'll see her alone and I don't want any mirrors in the room so you can watch us from the other side like we're too dumb to know you're there."

She stomped out of the room, leaving Susan's jaw hanging and me trying not to laugh. "Well, that's what I love about her," I finally said. "She's a tough cookie."

Susan was able to laugh at the situation too. "I guess if she can handle me, she can handle her mom."

And she did. Susan and I waited about 45 minutes before Marie opened the small conference room door and invited us in. "Look!" she exclaimed, holding up her mother's hand. "We've got the same hands!"

There was symbolism in that discovery for Marie. Her tiny hands and short fingers were so unusual in our family that Tony liked to say, "I've got toes longer than your fingers." Now she could hold her hand up to her mother's and they were exactly the same size. She found where she came from and where she belonged.

Of course, she wasn't moving back with her mother just because they had the same size hands. She wasn't moving back at all. DHS had long ago decided that Cheryl was not a fit mother. She had apparently made that decision for herself when she moved to North Carolina and gave her ex-husband custody. I know that must have hurt Marie at the time, but it didn't help when foster mother Cheryl told Marie that her mother had said to the judge, "I'm not letting these fucking kids ruin my life."

I wondered if that was an accurate quote, but beyond that why Marie needed to know it, even if it was. I got to know the real mom, as she and Marie began to visit once a month. I couldn't picture her saying that. She didn't even swear.

The visits started out at Agency A and quickly moved to mom's apartment in Biddeford over the corner store where she worked. Things went well for the most part. Mom and Marie were always happy to see each other and tearful when they parted.

My job was to transport and then to supervise, something I found very stressful. I was to steer the conversation away from certain subjects, primarily their shared past. And that required me to come up with ever more creative ways to change the subject.

All mom wanted to talk about was the past. She must have seen me as a willing listener, or perhaps wanted to punish me for interfering in her relationship with her daughter, but she often called me on the phone between visits and babbled on and on about the things that had happened to her. I listened but I found it annoying. I felt she was trying to justify something unjustifiable- deserting her children, and leaving them with an abusive man. I didn't think Marie should have to listen to that. So when I say I was instructed to steer the subject to the present, I don't mean against my will. I agreed with my mission at the time.

It seemed more productive for them to talk about Marie's school life, her horseback riding lessons, her friends and boyfriends. Happy talk. I pictured Marie calling her mother to ask advice about a boy or to commiserate about a difficult teacher. But that never happened. Now I look back and think about Maslov's Hierarchy of Needs. That concept helps me understand that certain needs have to be met before others. A person who is starving as well as uneducated will pursue food before he will pursue an education. It is just a more primary need. Marie and her mother had a primary need, one that had to be met before they could move on. That need was to understand how this happened to them, why they were mother and daughter yet their contact was limited to one supervised hour a month. But I did my job well. I never let them understand.

While Marie was enlarging her family, I was enlarging mine. I took in respite foster kids and occasional short-term foster kids. She wasn't always happy with it, but there was always an end in sight. One child was a girl just Marie's age who had come from the same small town of Waterboro. Her name was Monica. A permanent foster home was being readied for her. She just had to cool her heels with us for 3 months while the licensing process took place.

Marie and Monica didn't know each other before they met in my home because they went to different elementary schools. They would have met eventually in middle school, if Marie had stayed in Waterboro. Their best times were spent gossiping and comparing notes on people they knew in common from school and town. They begged to take a day off school to go walk through the halls and surprise their old friends. It sounded like fun to me, so we did it.

The visit to the middle school went so well that we decided to make one more stop and see Marie's sixth grade teacher, Mrs. Wood, at the elementary school. I knew she had been very involved with Marie in the last year before she moved in with me. I read notes of a meeting that the school had called with Agency A to discuss Marie's problems. Cheryl Reedy was at the meeting and the notes said that the teachers had been very hard on Cheryl and that she "felt attacked." I knew I was going to like this teacher. I also knew she would be happy to see Marie doing so well. She was so happy she cried.

After lots of hugging and jabbering about her new life, Marie flitted about, visiting other old friends around the school while her old teacher, Mrs. Wood and I talked. She told me that she had run into the Reedy family recently. When she got the chance she asked Linda how her sister Marie was doing and Linda said she didn't know, that they had lost contact. Mrs. Wood gave her a little lecture about the importance of keeping in touch with blood relatives and Linda leaned close and said, "I can't now. I've got to survive where I am. When I'm eighteen I'll find Marie."

I shared that information with Marie later when we were alone. So far, we had been told Linda wasn't interested in getting together with her sister. She was still angry about all the problems she'd cause at Reedys and all the "lies" she told. Marie never believed that any of that really came from Linda.

"That's Cheryl talking," she would always tell me. This information pretty much confirmed it.

"I told you, didn't I?" Marie said. "Linda doesn't have any choice how to act around Cheryl. She doesn't want to end up like me locked in her room. And she doesn't want to leave her school friends."

I called the social workers again the next day. We had our standard conversation about how there was nothing they could do unless Linda said to them what she was apparently saying to others. I knew that would be the response, but I wanted my information documented somewhere besides with me.

Then one day Linda called. Reedys were going out of town for the weekend and leaving her home alone. She wanted to know if she could see Marie. I drove happily to Waterboro to make that happen. If I'd ever had any doubt what went on at Reedys' I didn't any more after that weekend. It was clear from the minute the girls saw each other and hugged.

"I am so sorry," Linda said, but Marie didn't need an apology. She knew. Linda knew. They both knew the same truth of what had happened and the position each girl had been put in. There was no need to explain what they already knew.

The conversation went immediately to how much they both hated the Reedys. Linda told horror stories about the child who had taken Marie's place and how badly he was treated. Apparently, he was removed after a year and a formal abuse complaint was filed. Linda didn't know the outcome. The girls talked a mile a minute all the way back to Portland, jumping from subject to subject with the breakneck speed I was now accustomed to between Marie and her mother. They didn't seem to care that I was in the front seat taking in every word. Many of the details Marie had given me were confirmed by the conversation. Nothing at all was said about Marie's "bad" behavior nor was there any reference to the possibility that Marie's problems with Cheryl were her own fault.

I knew I would call the social worker yet again on Monday, but by now I knew it would go nowhere. I would be placated with some feigned concern and then told something that would shut me up for the moment. Something like, "Linda has a history of lying." or "Cheryl saved Linda's life once."

Social workers are very good at retelling a story to make it fit the plans they have already made. The example that finally opened my eyes to that was the Teen Support Group debacle.

One evening a month was support group time at the Agency A offices. There was enough room for 2 parent groups, a teen group and a little kid group. Marie had been in the little kid group when she moved in with me, but a year later she turned 14 and was old enough to move up to the teen group. She was really excited about that, mostly because Linda would be there. I didn't know until the evening was over that she had been shuttled back to the little kid group. She was extremely disappointed. I called Agency A the next day and asked why.

"All of the kids who turn 14 during the year move up together in September," I was told. That was months away.

I bought it. Marie didn't.

"Bullshit," she exploded when I told her. "I've been in that kid group for years. I watched kids go up to teen group the minute they turn 14. They just don't want me with Linda."

I kept that to myself for a while, but brought it up to Susan as we waited outside the conference room while Marie was reuniting with her mother. We were joined at that moment by Jean, Susan's boss, the one who actually told me that the kids move up all at once. They looked at each other when I asked the question, as if they shared a secret, and the pause was long enough to be very telling.

"Well," Susan finally said, "the truth is the teen group doesn't want Marie. They say she's too disruptive."

She might as well have added, "Yeah, that's the ticket." The kids in the teen group were plenty disruptive all by themselves, and many of them were boys dying to get a crack at Marie. But I was still shocked that she was admitting the first story was just that, a story.

"You lied to me!?" was all I got out before Marie summoned us in to see the size of her mother's hands. It was a stunning revelation to me. I never expected anything but honesty from Susan or any of the team members. How could we be a team without it? Marie was right. Cheryl was calling the shots, keeping the girls apart as long as possible.

That insight didn't stop me from calling the social worker with each new piece of information. I just stopped thinking that she actually wanted to know it, that she was actually interested in the truth. I knew by then the truth was irrelevant to her. I just wanted it documented that I knew.

CHAPTER 5

✦ ✦ ✦

Twenty-Seven Points

I chose Agency A because I saw their ad in the paper about the same time I was having my epiphany about not needing a man. It seemed like it was meant to be.

I met with the folks at Agency A and was favorably impressed. The people were warm, intelligent and pleasant. They explained that Agency A was a private social service agency who subcontracted with DHS. They were founded by two individuals who wanted to do a better job with foster kids than could be done by the state. They did this by providing more funding, but also by directing the money to the right areas. Their social workers were paid better than they would be by the state, so they were able to attract better people and keep them longer (in theory). They also felt strongly that foster kids should be well dressed so they could feel good about themselves. Agency A refunded for any money spent on clothes, instead of providing a limited stipend as DHS did. Together, DHS and Agency A handpicked children who might have the potential to remain in one placement for the rest of their childhood. Then everybody worked to make that happen.

I was thrilled with Agency A and they were happy enough with me to invite me to join. After a reasonable evaluation of my fitness and a 2-week pre-service training, I was ready to go. Then I met Marie.

Working with Agency A, I had minimal contact with Department of Human Services. Each child has a DHS worker and they remain ultimately responsible, even once Agency A gets involved. Marie had Don Reed, but his card in my purse was the only contact I had with him. For the most part I dealt directly with Agency A. When I wanted Marie to get special testing or to take private voice lessons, I wrote a letter to Agency A, they discussed it with the DHS worker and then I got the answer back from Agency A.

There was only one occasion when we all got together and that was the semi-annual Case Review. In the interest of time, Marie and Linda were always done together. So every 6 months I met in a small conference room in Biddeford with Cheryl Reedy, our Agency A social worker, Don Reed and his supervisor, Cal. The real parents were invited, but usually didn't make it. The supervisor would go through a prepared questionnaire, asking things like, "How are her grades? How does she get along with peers?"

I would brag a little about Marie, once calling her my lovable little firecracker. Cheryl would brag about Linda, her A student. Neither of us looked the other in the eye. I knew Cheryl called in reports when she heard Marie had been spotted smoking, just like I called in every time I learned something more about the abuse Marie suffered in the Reedy home. None of that came up in the case review. I left saying, "Phew! Done for another six months."

The case review was tense because Cheryl was there, but it didn't really amount to much. No advice was sought or given. No changes were made because of it. I considered it a technicality until the review in November of Marie's third year with us. That time was very different.

To begin with, few of the expected participants showed up. I sat there with Don and his supervisor, making small talk for a while. We peeked out into the waiting room every few minutes. Finally someone made a few phone calls and it turned out the others had either forgotten or been called away. So the three of us went on without them.

It started out like every other meeting. I answered all their questions, giving little anecdotes wherever I could to illustrate some point about Marie's progress. They were pleased as usual. Everyone always remarked on what a good move it was for Marie when she came to live with me. We were about to break up when the supervisor, thumbing through the file, came up with one more question.

"Have Marie and Linda seen each other?"

"Oh, yes, they're getting along fine now."

Eyebrows shot up. "Wow. How did that happen?"

"Linda apologized."

"For what?"

"For everything that happened. For not defending Marie."

"Defending her?"

"From Cheryl."

They stared at me. "I'm missing something," Cal said after a moment.

I felt a hot flush from my head to my toes. They didn't know. I had long since given up on anyone caring, but here were two key players who didn't have a chance to care. They didn't know. I considered back peddling, but I had gone too far.

"Marie was treated very badly at Reedys. She was kept in her room, excluded from family activities. She had no toys or books. She was never allowed to finish a meal so she was starving."

"How do you know all this?"

"Marie has been telling me about it, and Linda confirms it. She was just too afraid of Cheryl to stand up for Marie. She has apologized."

Don and Cal were appalled. "We have been led to believe that Reedys were exemplary foster parents. We were always happy when we were able to get a child in there," Cal told me.

"Marie has some horror stories about other kids who were treated just as badly there. She says the only time Cheryl was nice to her was when there was another child there she hated more. Some kid with cerebral palsy was the butt of some really cruel jokes, I'm told."

"Billy." Cal said. "I placed him there."

I shrugged. "I don't think she's making it up. As a matter of fact, I know she's not."

Cal and Don looked at each other with genuine dismay. "Why didn't you let us know sooner?" one of them asked. "Why is this just coming up now?"

"I've been talking to Agency A about it."

"No one ever said a word."

After more discussion, they asked me to do something for them. They asked me to sit down with Marie and have her list everything she could remember about living at Reedys. They asked me to take notes and send it to them.

Can open, worms everywhere. Marie and I went to Pizzeria Uno that evening and I filled a yellow legal pad with notes. She was ecstatic that someone was finally listening.

I typed it up later, listing each incident or issue separately. When I was done there were 27 points. They included all the rules around eating, the punishments for breaking them, the chores Marie had to do that no one else did. There were a number of things I hadn't heard before and I had to force myself not to start crying right there in Pizzeria Uno when she told them to me. I didn't know Cheryl had punished her by not allowing her to bathe for days at a time, or that when she did bathe her sister was assigned the chore of watching her to make sure she didn't masturbate. I didn't know that Cheryl had caught her putting Kleenex in her bra once and called the whole family in to see, and saying that Marie was a slut just like her mother. I didn't know she got a limited number of pads when she got her period each month and was punished if she "stole" more or made a mess in her underpants.

I mailed the list into DHS as I was asked to, but I also made another copy and mailed it to Agency A. I called Susan to warn her first. I felt bad for her because I had a suspicion she would be made a scapegoat for all this. Not because she let Marie be abused. She wasn't even around when that happened, but because she failed to keep me in line, because she wasn't at the Case Review.

I enclosed in both packets a series of pictures I had taken of Marie over the years. The first was taken before she even moved in with us. She was standing in the bright sun in her denim dress with the scrawniest little legs poking out. Her hair was dry and dull looking, her facial bones, sharp. The next was taken three months later on our vacation in New Mexico. Her hair was cut bluntly just below her chin, thick and shiny. Her face was soft and tanned, her limbs healthy looking. All of the rest of the pictures look solid and healthy, though admittedly there were none taken during her brief chubby phase. Even I was astounded looking at the physical change and just as astounded that it hadn't registered before. She was malnourished in the first picture. It is amazing what we can take for normal until we have something to compare it to.

34

I got a call from Agency A the next day. It was a conference call. The director was there, as were two other administrators, Glenn and Jean. They also introduced a lawyer. They started out being extremely polite, but were interested in how I came to make these notes. They wanted to know specifically who asked for the notes and who all I had talked to about making them. They finally got around to talking about Marie and how sorry they were to have missed the signs. I tried to be as polite as they were, but I had to point out that some of the people there were the very people who called me to complain that I was too nice to her, buying her a bracelet for Christmas and a dress for sixth grade graduation.

I pressed that point. "How could you have missed that there was something wrong when they wanted her to go to her own graduation in an old pair of pants?" I asked. "Doesn't Agency A's own philosophy say something about wanting these kids to fit in, not to wear rags because they are foster kids?"

I was surprised that the answer to that was ready. Maybe the file was out in front of him, but Glenn answered, "Reedys felt they had worked very hard to keep Marie's materialistic nature in check and that you were undoing all the good they had done."

"I would think you would have been calling Reedys, not me, saying let the kid wear something new. It was an important occasion."

"Well, it's all very clear now," Glenn said. "When you put the whole thing down like this…twenty-seven points. It's all pretty shocking put this way. But not when it comes a little at a time."

"It was to me." I said.

"Then why didn't you file a formal abuse complaint?" Paul, the director, interjected. He was done being polite. "You're a mandatory reporter too."

"I thought telling the social worker was reporting it. Why didn't somebody tell me if there was another avenue to take?"

"You didn't know there was a child abuse hot line? The number is displayed in public bathrooms all over the city. Everybody knows there is a child abuse hot line."

I was dizzy with the quick turn the conversation had taken. How did I become the bad guy? What was this conversation really about, shifting blame? And why the lawyer?

"She wasn't being abused any more."

"It doesn't matter. You should have reported it."

"Fine. I guess I'll do that now."

Later I realized I should have waited until Marie got home from school to call. Or let her make the actual phone call. But I was so angry I grabbed the phone book and dialed the child abuse hot line as soon as the conference call was over. She was okay with it when she got home.

She was handling the whole thing with a tangled mess of mixed emotions. Sometimes she was elated, feeling powerful at long last, and I felt I was doing the right thing by her. Then other times we would be talking about it, and she would start crying, reliving the pain and the impotent rage. I would hear her on the phone with friends later and realize she was taking her anger out on them. Her grades were slipping. I wondered if I should slowly let the subject drop and let her go on with her typical teenager life.

I asked her one day, "If this whole thing with Reedys goes exactly the way you want it to, how will it go? What is your fantasy? Do you want an apology? Do you want her to go to jail?"

"Oh, I know the answer to that one," she said with a smile. "I've been dreaming about it for years. I want to buy a gun and drive down there and shoot her."

That's when I knew I needed to press on, let her exact her revenge in another way, a legal way. I offered to get her a lawyer. The lawyer suggested I get her a counselor. To my surprise, Marie agreed to it.

Most kids go through life with parents, teachers, doctors and dentists. Some also have coaches and the occasional counselor. Foster kids have parents, foster parents, ex-foster parents, and respite foster parents. They have doctors, dentists and teachers who change every time the placement changes. They also have social workers, one from the state and one from their agency who always promise to stay and always break that promise. They have counselors and court appointed lawyers. Marie had now added a private lawyer to her list and welcomed a counselor back on to it. But she was boycotting her Agency A social worker.

Marie was always boycotting someone, but I didn't blame her this time. In her mind Agency A had failed her the most, though in truth, they had only failed her the most recently. I was in an awkward position because I was employed by Agency A, and yet I was taking Marie to a lawyer who might eventually help her sue them. I certainly couldn't share that or much else that was going on at home with our Agency A worker. So I was effectively shutting Susan out too, just more politely. The triangle was just too complicated for me. I needed an objective person to talk to, but one who was already on the inside. I called Don Reed, her DHS worker and he agreed to come out to the house to talk the whole situation out.

Don was a big, burly guy, a cop before he went into child protective work. That fact alone made him more of a straight shooter than any social worker I'd ever met. His impending retirement might have loosened his lips a bit too.

I went back to the beginning. "I don't understand why Marie never went back to her parents." I said. "Was there really just that one episode? Marie says she never got hit before that night."

"That was pretty much it. But her dad had a bad attitude. Always angry, threatening to sue. And Mom was always crying. They didn't make a very good impression on judges."

"Why did the boys go back and not the girls?"

"The boys were much harder to place. Older, not so cute."

"But if their home was dangerous, wouldn't it be dangerous to the boys too?"

"We had nowhere else for them. They kept causing trouble everywhere they went."

"Did the parents really take the classes and go to all the appointments they were supposed to go to? I mean, how do you justify keeping any of the kids if they have done all they've been asked to do?"

"They made one big mistake. They lied to the judge once. They went into court saying they were back together so it would seem like a more stable family, and we were able to prove they were lying."

"How long had the kids been in care by then?"

"A couple of years."

"How desperate would you be, if your kids were in foster care for two years and you had done everything right to get them back? I know I would lie, cheat and steal if I had to, if it meant getting my kids back."

Don had a reputation as a very good dad to his own kids. "I know," he said, shaking his head. "You're right. They should have gone home a long time ago." He paused. "The truth is the guy who had the case before me was eventually fired for his heavy-handed, punitive techniques. But they went back over his cases after he left. And as far as Marie and

Linda were concerned, it was determined that it was too late to go back and fix it."

I was almost too stunned to continue. "How can it ever be too late to get your kids back?" I asked. Of course in the back of my mind I was hoping it was too late now. I couldn't imagine losing Marie myself.

"We thought Linda and Marie were happy where they were."

"But Marie was telling people she was unhappy. She told counselors. I've seen the documentation. The counselors just called Cheryl and ratted on her. No one believed her."

"Well, Marie did have a history of lying."

"What history? I've heard dozens of stories, but none of them is of Marie lying, just of people not believing her."

"The whole thing that brought them in to care was about Marie lying."

"It was?"

"She said she shaved the cat. She didn't."

"That's it?"

Don looked embarrassed. "That's it," he said.

"That was one lie and it was to stop her dad from hitting. And for that she never got believed again?"

He looked even more embarrassed. "Yeah." Then he added. "She was refusing to see her mother by then. It didn't seem likely she wanted to live with her if she didn't even want to see her."

He had a good point. I made a mental note to ask Marie later why she quit seeing her mother and if she really ever said she was happy at Reedys. Her answers broke my heart. "Cheryl told me my mom had AIDS and I could catch it and die. I was, like, nine. I believed it. And Cheryl was always there when they asked if I wanted to stay with her. I couldn't say no. I was afraid I'd end up at that trailer home with 20 other kids picking through garbage."

There was one other thing Don told me. He didn't have to. I would have never thought to ask. He said there was a note on Marie's file stating that no one was to visit Reedys unannounced and that they weren't allowed to interview the children away from the foster mother.

"Who would have put a note like that on the file?"

"I don't know."

"Why would they have done it?"

"I can only assume the foster mother requested it."

My talk with Don opened my eyes in so many ways. Besides the truth about Marie's background, I learned the reality about private social service agencies. There was one on every street corner, with names like Kidspeace, Woodfords Child Care, and Maine Caring Families. How I ended up with the impression that Agency A was the only one, I'll never know. And it was possible to switch from one to the other. It seemed to me to be the only answer. Marie needed to be given some power over her own life. She should be able to quit Agency A if she wanted to.

It was awkward researching the other agencies when I already had a foster child. I thought I could do it without telling Marie's story, but I found it impossible. I needed to see the other agency's reaction to it. They needed to see who I was by my telling of it. Everyone seemed stunned that anything like that could ever happen. And they all seemed more than happy to take on Marie and me. I chose Agency B for the same reason I originally signed on with Agency A. I really liked all the people I met there. They said all the right things. I became enthused with the idea of working with them and with taking on even more kids.

Also in my researching the agencies, one comment was made by several sources. I was told that Agency B strongly supported the foster kids while some of the other agencies were more likely to support the foster parents. I had a flicker of a question in my mind about why it was necessary to choose one over the other. Couldn't you just support both? But I wanted an agency that seemed like it wouldn't have let Reedys get away with abusing Marie. I wanted someone who would support her. I didn't think I needed all that much support.

It was easy to sign on with Agency B. The hard part was signing off with Agency A. I was hoping to do it by phone. The phone call itself left me shaking. Paul, the director, was wild. He said nothing like this had ever happened before. I later learned it happened all the time. He said it was impossible to take Marie with me. I pointed out that I had already cleared it with DHS. He demanded that Marie and I come down to Agency A to meet with him. I said Marie was refusing to walk in the building anymore.

"I find that shocking," he said, "not just that she feels that way, but that you would support it."

"I'm just trying to respect her feelings. She's the victim here. I'm not going to force her to do something she doesn't want to do."

"Sometimes that's a parent's job."

"Not in this situation. We can meet anywhere else. Just not at Agency A."

He agreed to come to our house the next Wednesday. I was surprised when a car full of Agency A people unloaded in front of the house. It was going to be our territory, but they were going to outnumber us. I was nervous enough for myself, let alone for the tiny 15-year-old girl who sat cross-legged on the couch next to me for this. I needn't have been.

Marie was amazing. I expected to let her have her say, then excuse her to go upstairs. I didn't want her punished for her decision. I planned to defend her rights, stick to my guns, whatever I had to do. I barely had to say a word.

Three adults browbeat her as if she was a hostile witness in a murder trial. They refused to admit any abuse had happened, though they said they were sorry for "whatever she felt she had gone through." They belittled her, invalidated her feelings, and interrupted her. Paul leaned threateningly toward her from the rocking chair he had chosen to sit in, insisting that we all "leave this behind us and move on." It wasn't a request. It was an order. I kept trying to come between them and Marie, but she didn't need me. She held her ground.

"The only reason you are in my life at all is to protect me from abuse. Instead you put me right in the middle of it and left me there. I have decided to leave Agency A and I'm allowed to do that. It is my choice."

It went on forever. The same things were said over and over. It felt like a brainwashing attempt. I was on the verge of tears, just from so much hostility in my living room, but Marie just sat there, holding my hand and defending her position. Finally I said, "Enough!" for the last time and it registered. They agreed to go, but Glenn kept repeating on the way out the door, "I'm glad we've begun this dialogue. We'll meet again next week…"

"No we won't," Marie said. "No we won't."

We collapsed into each other arms when it was over. Later that night, I wrote them a quick note.

"Marie claims for all those years she was with Reedys, you never heard her cries for help. Today, you sat in my living room and again, you didn't hear a word she said. She said, 'You're fired.'"

There was one more meeting that had to take place before the move was complete and that was at DHS. It was billed as "just a formality." We needed to choose the right date to change the billing or some minor thing. It turned out a little different.

Agency A sent two people. DHS sent two people. I came alone. Picking the right date took about thirty seconds. Then the supervisor from DHS started going over the expenses they had covered for Marie since she had been in my home.

He had it all right in front of him, obviously prepared just for this meeting. He also had some statistics as to how much is spent on the average foster child her age. It seems Marie had been pretty expensive since she moved in with me, what with the horseback riding lessons and the summer camp for kids with learning disabilities.

Glenn from Agency A pointed out that she was the best-dressed foster child in his agency, implying I spent their money frivolously.

I could have said SO MUCH if I had been prepared for this to be a confrontation. But I am not a quick reactor, so the right responses didn't come to me till the drive home.

But I had gotten the point. They would all stick together. And this could be turned back on me at any time.

CHAPTER 6

✦ ✦ ✦

You're Supposed to Cry

Changing from Agency A to Agency B was not like, say, switching long distance carriers. It was more like moving from elementary school to high school except for the fact that it was a move made by choice. And I made the choice for more than one reason. First and foremost was Marie's need to say good-bye to Agency A, but there were other issues. Marie had other issues.

She wasn't just a poor, abused child and I wasn't just her savior. She was also, 90% of the time, a typical teenager and I was her mother/ nemesis. Even as we sat in her lawyer's waiting room, we were bickering about her latest violation of the rules.

"After this I'm gonna stay downtown and see if I can find some of my friends."

"No, you're not! You're grounded."

"For what?"

"Hello. You were out till two thirty in the morning Saturday. Your curfew is eleven."

"It wasn't my fault. No one would give me a ride home."

"Marie, you weren't even where you said you were going to be. I called."

"So? We left Heather's and went to Dunkin' Donuts."

"Where they don't have phones?"

42

"I didn't want to wake you up."

"Like I'd be asleep. Marie, I've been through all this before with Renee. I know all the excuses. The bottom line is you are responsible for being home by curfew. You are responsible for keeping me informed as to where you are."

"This is such bull…"

Then Carolyn would come out and we would head back into her conference room to talk about Marie's potential case, slipping back into our "poor child" and "savior" roles.

I had to deal with Marie's blossoming rebelliousness and I knew I couldn't deal with it on the phone from work. I needed to be home more and at work less. With Agency A, I had Marie and a full time job. With Agency B, I would have Marie, one or two more foster kids and work less that 15 hours a week. I chose this because Marie needed more supervision, but I didn't tell her that.

Agency B specialized in a different kind of child, one labeled Treatment Level, one with more problems. Those kids required more time and attention; therefore the rate of pay was high enough to allow a parent to stay home most of the time. It was really a career change for me. Nursing would become a sideline. Foster care was now my career.

Marie understood the change…sort of. We talked about it, but she wasn't really paying attention. Her mind was occupied almost exclusively by her social life so I was able to slip some of the details by her. She was mostly focused on not getting another foster child close to her age.

"Okay," she would tell me when I reminded her of the changes to come. "As long as we only take girls and they are under seven."

"Wrong, Marie. I will avoid kids within two years of your age, but that's it. You don't make the rules around here."

"It's not going to work unless they are girls. This is a girl house. You don't even play sports. And I want a kid young enough to look up to me."

"Look, when we got you I had specified a child under eleven. You were two years older and it worked out fine. It's not about the age or sex. It's about the individual. And I am the parent around here. I will make the final decision."

Even though she spent most of her time mad at me, I knew it would be hard for Marie to share me. It had been hard for Tony and Renee too. As much as they loved Marie, they admitted there were pangs of jealousy sometimes watching me focus so much energy on her. But they were able to rise above it. I was sure Marie would too. But I decided to improve my chance of success by doing something special with Marie alone, before other kids joined us. We took a nine-day vacation to the Bahamas and Orlando.

The trip went perfectly. We shopped, we sunbathed, and we rode roller coasters together. We bought every cheesy $10 photo taken of the two of us. The high point for me was Marie winning the limbo contest on the beach in the Bahamas. For her, it might have been the boys who kept riding their bikes by us to get a look at her in her white bikini. In any case, we came home closer than ever, and I came home ready to accept the challenge of another foster child.

I had quit my job, fixed up Renee's old bedroom with bunk beds, and changed the dining room into a playroom. I was anxious to get started. But where were all those kids desperate for a home? Six weeks went by without a single child referred to Agency B. I was picking up every shift I could get at the local hospitals in order to pay the bills. There weren't many and those available were not conducive to raising a teenager by any stretch of the imagination, but I couldn't go without an income.

I was getting frantic when I finally got the phone call about Stephen, a nine-year-old living in a group home looking for a long-term placement. His classification as a treatment level foster child was based on a history of sexual abuse and some acting out on that history that made him a potential danger to other kids his age. I drove to Sanford to meet him. A week later, he came for a weekend. The following Thursday, he moved in.

Months later Stephen would ask me, "Did Marie smile before I moved in?"

She truly never got over it. He brought her a gift on his weekend stay and she didn't say thank you. Once he moved in she harangued him mercilessly about every little thing he did. Typical was the day I heard her yelling at him in the kitchen.

"He's eating grapes out of a bowl," she complained when I intervened.

"What do you want him to eat out of?"

"He should be using a plate. We'll need those bowls for breakfast."

"We have at least twenty-four bowls, Marie. Leave him alone."

She stomped up to her room. Scenes like this played out every day. She yelled at him for walking too fast or too slow. It didn't matter how many times I reminded her that I was the parent. Ten seconds later she would yell at him for something else totally ridiculous. Once, when we were in the Old Port, he was skipping ahead of us and Marie yelled at him to stop skipping.

Even as I said, "Next you'll be hollering at him for standing still," she was shouting, "No loitering," as he had stopped to wait for us in a doorway up ahead. "It's against the law."

"Do you hear yourself, Marie?" I said. "Do you know who you sound like?"

"It is against the law!" she repeated angrily.

"You sound like Cheryl Reedy. I'm not going to let you treat him like she treated you."

Lord knows, it didn't seem like the right moment for another child to move in, but I had very little choice in the matter. Six weeks without an income after an expensive vacation left me in a disastrous state financially. Tina was 11, thus a playmate for Stephen and possibly an admirer for Marie. I knew it wouldn't solve any problems. I just hoped I could control the ones it created. And in truth, it probably solved more than it created. Steve and Tina were best of buddies when they weren't battling siblings, which was completely normal as far as I could tell. And Marie's nagging was now divided between the two of them, so neither took it too personally, or for that matter, paid any attention to her at all.

But nothing was going to stop her.

"If Tina walks in my room one more time I'm going to deck her."

"You're not going to deck anybody. You have a bowl of Jolly Roger candy on your stereo. What do you think two little kids are going to do?"

"That candy is for my friends."

"You never have friends over. You're always out with Tristan."

Marie had developed a romantic relationship with a neighborhood kid whom I originally thought was adorable. But that was in middle school. By high school he had become emaciated and pale, wearing a heavy coat and stocking cap even in the summer, even in the house.

"What's wrong with him?" I'd asked her tactlessly.

"Nothing. It's a look."

"What? Homelessness? Heroin chic?"

45

"No. Everyone dresses like that."

I wouldn't have minded the look alone, but he had a reputation, and with Renee's old friends, I had the connections to know what it was. Druggy. One evening he came by the house for her, obviously stoned. Fortunately, Tony was visiting, so it wasn't my observation alone. Tony asked him to leave. Then he harassed us by phone for the rest of the evening, swearing at me, slurring his words like a drunk as the answering machine took message after message.

Marie was mortified when that happened and swore she had broken up with him over it. After she moved out a few months later, there was a picture of the two of them kissing on the front page of the high school newspaper accompanying an article on the pros and cons of public displays of affection. I can only assume they never really broke up and that was part of her motivation to get away from me.

Though I'd told Marie and both of her parents what I had learned from Don Reed, I never asked Marie if she wanted to go home. I didn't want to lose her. Plus the answer seemed obvious. Her life was with us now. She adored Tony and Renee, and if she wasn't always crazy about me, she was quite used to our lifestyle. She expected a room of her own, clothes bought at Club 21 and private lessons of one sort or another most of the time. She hadn't spoken to her father in quite a while and had grown most intolerant of her mother's incessant babble. Neither had a spare room for her anyway if she had decided to go back.

So I never expected her to leave no matter how bad things got between us. It was just mother/daughter stuff, I thought, the same sort of thing I had gone through with Renee.

Marie's maternal grandfather died that summer and I took her to the funeral. All four siblings were there, Matt and Randy, Linda and Marie. Besides Marie's parents, there were aunts and uncles I'd never met, some of whom were quite delightful. The grandparent's home was a well-kept old farmhouse in a nice middle class community. It all seemed so achingly incongruous. Why did these kids have to bounce around the foster care system when there was a home and a family like this that they belonged to? They weren't a perfect family. There were divorces and drinking problems. But there was a grandfather that Marie hadn't seen since she was six and now would never see. There were cousins who were complete strangers.

Marie started to sob, great gulping sobs, the minute we walked into her grandparents' home and didn't stop until we pulled into our driveway many hours later. I asked, but she couldn't articulate why she was crying. Just as she could never articulate why she was angry whenever she was angry with someone in her family, which seemed to be constantly.

I thought of the hours, years actually, she had spent sitting on her bed in her barren room at Reedy's supposedly thinking about how bad she was. If I were a little girl in that situation I'd be thinking about my real parents and using my magical mental telepathy to tell them to come and get me. Then as the years passed I would grow angry and bitter that they cared so little that they never came. I thought that anger was the thing she felt but couldn't articulate. I wondered myself why none of them had come to her rescue. I learned later that all had tried and been deemed "unfit" by DHS. But all Marie knew was that no one came when she needed them. I thought that disappointment was the real reason for her tears at her grandfather's funeral. Of course, she denied it.

"It's a funeral. You're supposed to cry," she snarled on her way upstairs. And that was the end of that.

Things continued to deteriorate, no matter how insightful I thought I was. The issues were beginning to pile up. Marie was sneaking around and getting caught at it regularly. She was trying her best to make life miserable for Steve and Tina. And she was failing Spanish.

That might not seem like such a big deal for a kid who is known to be a poor student, but I was taking her to a Spanish tutor once a week and paying for it myself. I bought her audiotapes and listened to them with her whenever we were in the car. And when I got the call from her school counselor that she was failing Spanish I offered to meet with her teacher to see what else we could do about it.

"She doesn't even come to class most of the time," he told me, "and when she does she acts like she's better than anyone else." I flipped!

That played right into the Driver's Ed issue. Marie was determined to learn to drive and I repeated over and over. "I have to see a pattern of mature behavior before you're going to get behind the wheel of my car. I don't consider cutting Spanish class mature behavior." She flipped.

There are real issues, like Marie's real family. There are semi-real issues like Marie's boyfriend and her grades. And there are pseudo-issues. Those are the ones we create to distract us from the real issues or justify our decisions in ways that are less painful than the real issues would allow.

Our pseudo-issue was Marie's increasing propensity to take and use my things as if they were her own. In the past she had done it once in a while. Renee did it too. When one of my sweaters or a pair of earrings was too tempting they just helped themselves to it, thinking they would put it back before I found out, then forgetting. It always drove me crazy, partly because if they had asked, I would have said yes, but mostly because it showed such disrespect.

It happened every few weeks, maybe once a month that I would look into Marie's room and there would be my sweater on her floor. But in the months before she left, it happened with such frequency that it had to be deliberate. Marie's last weekend, for example, went like this.

On Saturday Marie went skiing. I was home when she got dressed and there to say good-bye. That night I looked everywhere for the heavy socks I wore to bed at night. They were nowhere to be found until I checked Marie's dirty clothes hamper.

I had purchased new deodorant for myself that day and put it in the cabinet in the bathroom. The next morning, before I even had a chance to confront her about my socks, I got out of the shower to discover my deodorant missing. I stomped into Marie's room and opened her backpack. There it was.

"Why is my deodorant in your backpack?"

"Oh, I need it for gym."

"If you need deodorant, say so. You don't just take mine."

"I was gonna pay you for it."

"I didn't buy it for you. I bought it for me and you have no business taking it. And how did my brown socks get into your dirty clothes hamper?"

"I wore them skiing."

"I WAS RIGHT HERE!!!!" I said as loudly as one can say something without screaming it. "Why didn't you ask?"

"I don't know."

"I have had it! I am instituting a system of fines for taking my things. It's going to cost you $5 every time. This is going to stop!"

She turned around and walked away as she did moments into every argument.

"Don't you dare walk away when I'm talking to you!" was a frequent refrain of mine. She would turn back around with her hands on her hips, allowing me to say one more thing, and then she would walk away again.

That was the Sunday morning before she left. That evening, Steve was showing her the L.L. Bean socks I had just purchased for him. They were thick and forest green with the words L.L. Bean across the toes. I walked in the room.

"Marie's gonna buy my socks from me," Stephen said happily.

"I don't think so," I answered.

"Why not?" he whined.

"Well, first of all they're not yours to sell. I paid for them. And I bought them because you needed socks." Marie was standing right there and I directed the next comment to her. "If you like them, they are on sale at the outlet downtown. You can pick up a pair on your way to work this week."

The next morning, Stephen cheerfully showed me his newly acquired $6. "I'm buying candy on my way to school."

"Where did you get the money?" I asked, already suspecting the answer.

"Marie paid me for my socks."

"When?"

"When you were in the shower."

I took the six dollars and fumed all day. My anger grew with every passing moment. She may not have known what she was walking into when she got home from school that day, but she should have. The words L.L. Bean were poking out of the toe end of her sandals. I didn't even waste time pretending to care how her day went. I just blew.

We yelled at each other for a good thirty minutes. I yelled about the socks, the deodorant, the other socks as well as her grades and her recent lies about when she was working and when she wasn't. She yelled that I treated her like a baby not letting her take Driver's Ed, checking up on her whereabouts all the time. She walked away four times in the middle of the fight and I followed her each time, until she tried walking into the bathroom while I was talking. I grabbed the doorknob and yanked the door out of her hands as she was closing it, then took her upper arm and spun her around to where she was facing me again.

"You will not move until I am done talking. Do you understand me?"

She looked stunned and stood where she was until I finished, uttering no further response. It was the first time I ever laid a hand on her in anger and to this day I don't regret it. I would have done the same thing to Renee in the same situation. But it was the end. Three years and eight months after joining our family, Marie rejoined her own.

I found out she was gone when I got back from Stephen's karate class later that afternoon. She left a note on the kitchen table. I thought it must have felt good for her to be comforted by her own family for once.

I didn't go looking for her. I didn't call around. I waited until the next day to let DHS know. They found she was living with her aunt Cindy, going to the same high school, and still hanging around with the same friends. DHS agreed she was too old to try to force back to a foster home. We all decided to leave well enough alone.

I cried for three days and then I woke up the fourth morning and said to myself, "Thank God!" She was never really mine and, on some level, I'd always known it.

I guess it's easier to say, "Fuck you. I'm leaving." than "I love you, but it's time for me to go."

Her interdepartmental complaint, the one I called in, took over a year to investigate and in the end was deemed "Unsubstantiated." Susan called to let me know when that verdict was in. She said Linda failed to corroborate Marie's story. Linda, who was by then living with her boyfriend, said she not only agreed with everything Marie said but she added more details.

There are several pictures of Marie still on my mantelpiece. The best is a one we took right before prom freshman year. Her hair is piled up on her head in curls, a sparkly red dress picks up the light from the window and the look on her face says the future is unlimited.

I hope that is true for her. If not, there is a note pinned up for her at the local teen homeless shelter with our new address and phone number.

Tina

I ran into Nicole one day at a Agency A function. I was stunned, as the last time I saw her she was tearing up my house. Plus, I had been told she was in a locked psychiatric unit out of state.

She and I had nothing to say to each other, but I soon cornered a social worker, anxious to find out what happened.

That's when I learned that, after years of running away from group homes and psychiatric units, always heading straight for her grandmother, Nicole was allowed to move back in with the woman.

"I thought Grandma was considered a bad influence on her," I said, confused.

"No one else would take her."

CHAPTER 7

✦ ✦ ✦

Rough Handling on the Way to the Car

Whenever Marie brought up her desire to have only girl foster children in our home and only young ones I would say, "It's not like there is some catalogue to pick from." Turns out I was wrong. There is almost a catalogue. It is actually a stack of referrals on the desk in the Intake office at Agency B. Ann Ouelette is the Intake worker and once she got to know me I was allowed to come down to her office and go through the stack whenever I wanted to.

It was a strange experience. Getting a new child is weird enough as it is, as I told my foster mom friend Carol when I got Stephen, "I feel like I'm giving birth to a nine-year-old." This is especially true when you see yourself as doing "long term" foster care as I did. My goal was to primarily take kids who needed a growing up home, not kids who need an emergency or temporary placement. I ended up taking those sorts of kids sometimes, mostly when they begged me. But when I got Stephen and when I went through the stack of referrals and found Tina, I was looking for a keeper.

So it makes sense to pay attention to the details and pick a child you think you can enjoy for a long, long time. It's hard to say what I was looking for when I went through the stack. It would be ridiculous to hold out for a child without problems. I was in Therapeutic Foster Care. The perfect child wouldn't be in that stack. But there were a few things that ruled kids out so they were put in the "Don't Even Think About It" pile. As an old burn nurse, or perhaps just as a normal human being, I didn't want to live with a fire starter. I knew a child with overt sexual acting out behavior wouldn't be appropriate with the two I already had. And I'm not good with depression. I was married to a depressed man. Flashbacks of Richard on the couch with the drapes pulled saying, "Life sucks and then you die," would put me in a non-therapeutic mind-set for sure.

So I sat at the table and read through the psyche evaluations and social worker interviews and made two piles. Once I was done I would talk to Anne about all the kids in the "Maybe" pile and get more insight. Sometimes the worker who called her had dropped a tidbit of information that was not in the written material. Sometimes the child was already placed, which was really a bummer if that one had started to tug at my heartstrings already.

When I got to Tina in the pile, I laughed out loud as I put her paperwork in the "Don't Even Think About It" pile. Anne looked up from her work with a quizzical expression.

"Oh, this little Tina," I explained, "three assault charges and a breaking and entering. She's never going to find a home."

"Well, actually," Anne said, "her DHS worker loves her. She says all those behaviors reflect the environment she lived in, not the child. She's been in an emergency foster home for a while and they love her too."

Okay, back to the "Maybe" pile for Tina.

"Her worker said if she herself was younger she would get into foster care just to get Tina."

To the top of the "Maybe" pile.

In the end, Tina, at eleven, was the youngest in the Maybe pile, which I thought might help sell her to Marie and she had the stamp of approval from people who had actually spent time with her. I now looked at her behavior history as a challenge instead of an impediment. My maternal instinct and my hero complex were both shifting into gear. That's another one of the things I've learned about myself and about doing foster care. If either or both of those instincts are triggered by a particular child, I can put up with a lot. If I can't really feel something, there is no point in even trying, at least not with long-term kids.

When I finally met Tina, I wondered how she ever triggered anyone's maternal instinct. She was clinging to her birth mother and whimpering when I was introduced, saying good-bye after one of her weekly supervised visits. I looked past her at first, for a girl, thinking the clinging child a boy. When I realized my error, I hoped my surprise didn't show.

Tina was eleven, but had the size and potbelly of a much younger child. There is no gentle way to describe her features. She had bug eyes, a flat nose and no neck. Her hair was cut short and her voice deep. I looked up at her mother for the genetic source and found none. Must be Dad, I thought. Poor Tina.

But Stephen was with me and zeroed in on something else. They had the exact same hair color and cut. "We're twins," he cried, and they ran off into the nearby woods, lovely with fall foliage, for a game of hide and seek. After a brief awkward conversation with mom, I went off in search of the two of them for our hour long unsupervised visit.

Steve was running back towards me as I crossed the small bridge that lead to the woods.

"She knows the rules already," he whispered excitedly. "She said 'we have to go back. They can't see us over here.'"

"You like her, don't you?" I asked.

"Oh, yeah," he exhaled.

Tina had pretty much passed the audition at that point, so I took her to see our house and neighborhood, instead of to the local McDonald's. She was delighted and fired questions at me when she wasn't wrestling and tickling with Stephen.

"Where will I go to school? Are there kids in the neighborhood? Will I have my own room?"

The last question was a yes, you will, but I won't. With one bedroom turned into a kid TV room, there were only three bedrooms left in our house. Steve and Tina couldn't share, even though he had bunk beds because they were not the same sex. Marie would have bolted even sooner if I tried to room Tina with her. So I had to give up my room and sleep downstairs in the playroom. I hung a curtain over the door and bought a really comfortable air mattress from a camping store for the floor. It wasn't so bad, I told myself, until it got crowded.

Tina had a habit of waking up and getting into bed with me, or onto the mattress to be quite literal. I sleep on my side, so she would slip in quietly and curl up facing me, usually gripping the front of my pajamas for dear life. It didn't take long for my over-the-counter sleeping pill to wear off and my shocked, sleepy self to shoot out the other side of the blankets peeling her off me as I went.

"What the heck...? Tina, you can't sleep with me. There is no room." Not only that, but sharing a bed with foster children is strictly forbidden, though I wasn't going to get into that in the middle of the night. I couldn't even stay long enough for her to fall back to sleep, as I might have done with one of my own. I could end up charged with sexual abuse.

It became a nightly nightmare. I tried sitting with her until she fell back to sleep, but she never did. I laid down on the couch in that room (which is also a licensing violation, by the way), but she climbed up with me. I tried to discuss it with her in the light of day, this time mentioning the legal aspects of things, but she erupted into this devilish cackle and dropped to the floor as if being tickled. She didn't want a night-light, never claimed to be afraid of the dark or to have nightmares. It began to seem as if it was a game to her, a moment in our lives when she was in control and I was helpless. I finally ended up just demanding that she stay in her own bed. She would be grounded the next day if she got into bed with me again. She did it anyway.

It's really hard to stay sane after enough sleep deprivation. I marched her back upstairs and sent her into her room and when she ran back out I yelled, "NO!!" blocking the doorway and pointing to her bed, glaring. She tried to leave her room again and I yelled even louder.

By this time Steve and Marie were coming out of their rooms to check out the commotion, mumbling their complaints and questions.

"Get back in bed," I demanded of the entire crew. Two of them had enough sense to do it and do it quickly. Tina continued the Mexican standoff. We stared silent daggers at each other. Then she finally turned around and got into bed.

"Do not let me hear your feet touch the floor," I said slowly enunciating each word. "Is that clear?"

"Yeah, bitch," she answered, enunciating equally well. I went back downstairs trembling with rage.

But that was Tina, one moment sweet and childlike, wanting to have a birthday party for her doll, the next day drawing tattoos on her arms to look tough for her probation officer.

Tina's DHS worker was more surprised to hear about the doll birthday party than the swearing and tattoos. She was happy to know that side of Tina existed. She said poor Tina was finally having the child-hood she had been denied in her former life, being practically forced out on the street by her neglectful parents. Lillian thought it was great that we actually had that party.

And what a party it was! It was an all day affair.

We cleared the garage, set up a table and chairs. We made decorations and then hung them. The kids made presents and wrapped them. Then we went to the store to buy a birthday cake. Sandy, the doll, had to be kept entertained by one of us at all times so she wouldn't figure out what was going on. Tina wanted her really surprised. Stephen asked me if I thought Tina knew she was just a doll and I said, "I think so," but I was less sure when I reached my spending limit in the grocery store and Tina threatened a fit.

"We need candles and paper plates and cups and a cake and ice cream…" she insisted as she hurried through the store gathering.

"Wait a minute," I said. "We have plates and cups at home."

"But they have to say Happy Birthday on them."

"No they don't. I've spent enough on this already."

Her jaw clenched and tears welled up in her eyes.

"No," she said anxiously. "We haven't even bought her presents yet."

"We made her presents."

"But we have to buy her real presents too."

"No, Tina. Enough, already. I will buy cake and ice cream. But we're going to have to pretend for the rest." Trying for a little parenting genius, I said, "Sandy's too young to know whether the plates say Happy Birthday or not. She can't read yet."

Tina paced up and down the aisle, her eyes downcast. Good thing she doesn't have a paper clip, I thought to myself. One of Tina's assault charges was based on an incident in school where she opened up a paper clip and jammed it into her teacher's arm. I gather it went in pretty far.

"Keep this up and we can skip the cake and ice cream too," I said, threatening being the only real genius.

"Okay," she said, brightening up as if nothing ever happened. "Let's go pick out her cake."

By now I knew better than to believe everything I heard about a child's past, but much of Tina's was a matter of public record, sometimes with newspaper accounts. She had attacked her teacher with the paper clip. She bit a school worker who was trying to restrain her. And she heaved a half empty liquor bottle she found across the playground at another child's head. All three victims needed medical treatment in an emergency room. She had also broken into an apartment in her neighborhood to steal a bike. Her side of that story was that it was a bike stolen from her friend in the first place and she was getting it back. Tina's rages at school had been so severe that once, instead of restraining her, they had cleared the classroom of other students and then called the police. She was also found once "partying" with a group of teenagers in motel room and another time, sleeping in a cardboard box with a homeless woman.

Lillian, her DHS worker, said her parents hadn't even bothered to look for her. She said Tina's behavior at school was thought to be, in part, the result of sleep deprivation as she shared a bedroom with her older sister's baby who was up a lot during the night. There was also the suspicion of abuse based on Tina's behavior, but they weren't able to bring charges until a teacher witnessed "rough handling" on the part of her stepfather one of the times he had to leave work because she was being suspended from school.

"That must have happened a lot from what you're telling me," I said.

"That was the fortieth time," Lillian said matter-of-factly.

"Wow," I commented. "I can't imagine how I'd handle my child if I was called to school for the fortieth time."

"It wouldn't happen to you. You'd have raised them better." Hmmm.

I had met Tina's mother that one time and she impressed me primarily as tired. She had long graying hair and the face of someone who had worked the night shift for too many years, maybe as a cocktail waitress. I was surprised when I later learned she was a lot younger than me. I wouldn't have guessed it.

She had weekly supervised visits with Tina that had to be rescheduled now that Tina was with me and I was with Agency B. It was my caseworker Pam's responsibility to set up those visits, as well as to visit Tina weekly, as she had Steve when he first moved in. His visits were now down to monthly, as he had been with me for four months.

She did manage to see each of them right on schedule, but that was about all Pam did. Agency A had disappointed me in their handling of Marie and her claims of abuse. But at least I felt I was dealing with grown-ups. Pam was just out of college. Agency B was her first job. She had no children of her own. And she took them to McDonalds every visit and let them play on the playground equipment. Sometimes she climbed around with them. Even Steve found that embarrassing.

"She what?" I asked when he confided in me.

"She plays with us, chases us around on the tunnels."

"She fits?" I asked. Pam was not a small person.

"Just barely."

I had to stop by McDonald's myself and take a look. I was sure there was a sign with an age or at least weight limit for playing on the jungle gym. There was. She was over it.

She also gave them gum at every visit as part of their ritual. Every person who saw them, be they family member or professional, had some ritual that involved buying them something. Their rooms overflowed into the hallways with "stuff" they had acquired. I should have been happy that, with Pam, it was only gum, but I had banned gum from the house after the last time I had to clean it out of the dryer and Pam knew that. The kids thought that was extremely cool that she defied my wishes. They loved to run in baring their teeth to show the gum when they came back from a visit. Pam would grin sheepishly in the background as if she tried to resist but just couldn't help herself. Then I would ask when Tina was going to see her mother and Pam would explain why it wasn't going to be this week, but possibly the next.

This went on for nine weeks. Tina's joy with the gum turned to tearful rage after each visit.

"Why?" she would beg me. "Why can't I see my mother?"

"Pam was sick this week and she didn't have time." or "Pam said your mother didn't return her call," or "You need to ask her yourself. I don't understand it either."

"You can take me, can't you?"

At that point foster parents did not supervise family visits. Social workers did. Later that would change. But I couldn't stand it any more myself. It was a Friday evening. Pam had canceled her own visit by phone, and rescheduled for the next morning. But Tina had grabbed the phone and asked if she was going to see her mother the next week. The answer was no and she was in tears again. I relented.

"Okay," I said. "I will try to reach your mother. If she agrees, I will take you to see her tonight. But you have to promise me one thing."

Steve was jumping up and down with anticipation right along with Tina. "This goes for you too, Steve. You have to let me tell Pam. Not you. Me."

"Okay, we promise," Steve assured me.

Tina's answer was obvious as she was rolling on the floor laughing. "I'm gonna see my mom. I'm gonna see my mom," she chanted.

"Don't get your hopes up yet," I told her. "No one else seems to be able to get her on the phone. I might not either."

I dialed the number Tina gave me. Her mom answered. And we hopped in the car and drove twenty miles to a Dunkin' Donuts.

I supervised from across the room. Steve and I had cocoa, Tina's mom's treat, and visited with each other. Periodically he would run over and hug Tina and her mother, who were hugging each other. He was clearly living vicariously through Tina, but I was impressed that he didn't demonstrate jealously. He would have loved to see his own mother. But he was happy for Tina and so was I.

I've been told I'm an unusual foster parent because I don't feel competitive with the birth mothers. Probably because I've already raised my family, so I don't need the kids to see myself as a mother. I am able to share them with their real mothers. I sometimes wish I could live next door to their mothers, so they could get what they need from me, safety and material goods, but run next door for the one thing I can't give, unconditional love. Though I would never say it to a child, on some level they must know that I would return them like a sweater that didn't fit under certain circumstances. Those circumstances could be behavioral, financial, even health.

If I was diagnosed with cancer, the kids would move on and contact would be lost almost immediately. The new foster home would want that and I would probably be relieved. That is why I always feel funny when foster kids say, "I love you." And they say it all the time, usually within days of moving in. It would be cruel not to say it back, but it is rarely true, at least at the beginning. Everyone deserves someone in his or her life who really means it. That's usually the real family in my experience, no matter what they did or didn't do to lose the child to the state.

Saturday morning, when both kids were dressed and anxiously awaiting Pam's arrival I reminded them of their promise.

"Remember, I will tell Pam in my own time. You keep your mouths shut."

"Okay, we promise, okay."

An hour later they came barreling in the front door screaming and giggling. Tina announced in her loud man voice, "He told! Stephen told!"

"No I didn't," he countered.

"Yes, you did!"

"Well, she asked."

Pam was not happy and I was mortified.

"I'm just concerned that you told them to keep a secret from me," she said. "Keeping secrets is a dangerous practice."

Shut up, you moron, I said in my head, but out loud I said, "I told them to let me tell you myself. It's not like you weren't going to know. But this has gone on way too long. Nine weeks."

"Well her mother doesn't return my calls," she defended herself.

"I had no trouble getting her on the phone," I said. I didn't add that her mother said she did return calls, but always got voice mail.

We smiled, phonies through and through, and said our pleasant good-byes. She said she would set up regular visits as soon as possible and get back to me.

When Pam left, I asked Steve what question she could possibly have asked that made him tell her about our visit to Tina's mother.

He hemmed and hawed but Tina barked, "She asked, 'What's new?' and Steve said 'Mary took Tina to see her mother last night.' We weren't even in the car yet."

Maybe Steve was jealous after all.

CHAPTER 8

✦   ✦   ✦

Rough Handling in the Parking Lot

Later Pam called and said Tina would be meeting with her mother every Friday at 1:30 P.M. starting that week, at the Agency B office and that I would need to drive her there and pick her up.

"I can't do it on Fridays," I said. "I work in the Emergency Room on Fridays."

"I believe it's in your contract," she said, curtly.

"Well, it's not in my calendar," I answered.

"Check your contract," she reiterated.

"It's in my contract that I can work 15 hours a week and I work on Fridays."

"That's the only day our family room has an opening," she explained.

"Then maybe you can pick her up from school and make the drive be your weekly visit." We only lived 2 miles from the meeting place.

"I don't think that would be an appropriate use of my time."

And burying yourself in colored ping-pong balls at McDonald's is? I screamed in my head, but I only verbalized, "I guess Tina won't be there," and ended the conversation.

I then marched over to the computer and did something I do well, but try to save for the right occasions. I wrote a letter to her supervisor.

The letter resulted in a meeting and ultimately a new worker, but I was told the new one would be no different from the old; that it was an entry level job, that they were all young and green and wouldn't be there very long. I needed to lower my expectations. I said I felt like I was raising my social worker as well as my foster kids and the big boss agreed that was partially true. The ride situation was not discussed, but another meeting was set up with the new worker and another supervisor so we could get off on the right foot. I could only hope!

My foster mom friend Carol gave me some insight into the "It's in your contract" comment. She'd been a therapeutic level foster parent for a lot longer and was well aware of the resentment for us among social workers. I was oblivious. I thought we would be considered valuable because we were willing to take the most difficult kids, to make a career of taking care of these children. I was shocked to hear that many considered us "over-paid whores." Apparently we make more money than the social workers do.

I've had friends visibly pale at the mention of money and foster parenting in the same sentence. Nobody wants to believe we "do it for the money." As a matter of fact "doing it for the money" is the polar opposite, in the eyes of the public, of doing it for the kids. I understand their feelings because of my acquaintance with the Reedys.

But I have spent my life as a critical care nurse. I've pumped chests, successfully saving lives. It's tremendously rewarding work. But I still take home a paycheck. I even concern myself with how big that paycheck is, considering it when I take a job, fighting for it when it is time for a raise. Doing good work doesn't exempt anyone from paying bills. Nuns and priests still have to pay their electric bill. Why would the electric company, the mortgage company or anyone else look kindly on me because I do foster care? They just expect to be paid. I expect to be paid. And I concern myself with how much I get paid.

How much do I get paid? Let's say I can replace a full-time nurse's salary with one therapeutic level child and one family level child, i.e. Steve and Marie. If I have that plus a second therapeutic level child, Tina, I take home much more than I did as a nurse.

How much do I spend as a foster parent? A fortune. At first I couldn't understand it. I thought when I took in Marie it would help pay the house payment. While the mortgage payment was due a few days after the foster parent check arrived, allowing me the illusion that one was paying the other, it wasn't. Every parent knows children have expenses.

What I didn't know was how much more expenses foster children have, especially if you do it right.

First, there is making them feel welcome when they arrive. I always let them pick out a new bedspread, decorate their room a little bit to make it their own. They usually come with very little clothes so we go to Susan's or Sears to try to dress them up for their first week of school. I get paid back for some of that, but I want them to look really good, so I usually go over my allotted funds. There are things like backpacks and clock radios most kids have accumulated in life, but foster kids come without. I have bought things like clock radios and even stereos for the kids' rooms, making it clear they belong to the room not the child, so I won't have the expense again with the next child. But they are always broken by the time the next child comes. I can't bring myself to show a child who is already sad or afraid his new room and have it barren or furnished with broken junk.

And speaking of breaking things. Marie broke an $850 lamp that I had taken a year to get out of layaway. Tina broke an end table and another nice lamp. Steve broke so many things I can't even name them all. The girls broke things because they had too much nervous energy, or because they were careless. Steve just loved breaking things. He would sit at my vanity in front of my jewelry box and snap the backs off of earrings just for fun. Once he threw my camera out the car window. It was the same camera I'd paid $75 to have repaired after Marie broke it.

Then we have utility bills. I know I shouldn't generalize, but most foster kids I've had need to have lights, music and fans on in their rooms all night. The electric bill skyrockets. They call their old friends or siblings on the phone and I feel I have to let them. A few months after Marie moved in I got a phone bill of $330. I put gas in the car every other day getting them to all their appointments.

Lastly we have entertainment. Most foster kids have never been to a restaurant besides McDonald's, or a museum or a live show. They haven't gone to all the great family festivals and county fairs this part of the country is famous for. Admittedly, they don't complain about it or beg to go to these things. I just can't resist the look on their faces when we get there. Maybe this is one thing I do for me as much as for them, but sometimes it functions as the positive reinforcement for good behavior. And sometimes a movie is better for all of us than staying home and watching them break things.

Okay, there is one more item. I don't mean to nit-pick but I had to have work done to the house to pass the fire inspection required to be a foster parent. I paid to have someone add a set of stairs to the back porch and reinforce the railings. I had to have an electrician add more electrical outlets. I bought bunk beds to have more sleeping space.

So, am I an overpaid whore? I don't think so. My credit card bills have only gone up since I started doing foster care. Way up. It got so bad, just a few months ago I sold my house and moved to a smaller, cheaper one. It has a better yard and more kids in the neighborhood, but the real motivating factor was financial necessity.

But if I complain to a social worker about my utility bills or repair bills they may well be thinking, "That's why you get the big bucks," or "I believe it's in your contract."

Eventually, I drove down to Agency B to meet my new worker and have the meeting about how we would work together. They made sure her supervisor was present so I wouldn't overpower her. I got there for the meeting and neither individual was in their office. I stood at the front desk perplexed for a few minutes.

"Are they at lunch?" I asked. "I mean, should I sit down and wait?"

People looked at each other. "Well, I thought I heard Karen say she had a home visit this afternoon...someone named Mary."

"I'm Mary, and it was not a home visit."

"Karen and Lesley left together for a home visit."

My patience was gone. I drove back home on the verge of tears I was so angry. I never would have agreed to have the meeting at my house. I might have cleaned a little if I'd planned to have it there, but I write down every word during phone conversations. I knew exactly what was said. When I got home and saw them sitting in their car in front of my house, I was not polite.

When we got in the house and I spread my weekly calendar out in front of them, demonstrating that I had 21 times a week that I had to get a child somewhere or pick them up on time, I was still not being polite.

Karen, the supervisor, suggested I look again at some of those appointments and prioritize.

"You want me to cancel some of them? Which ones? Marie's tutoring? Stephen's karate?"

"Well karate may not be the highest priority..." Karen said.

"Karate has done more for Stephen than his counselor has. Maybe I should cancel the counselor."

"That is mandatory."

"Maybe I should cancel Tina's probation officer. Oh yeah, that's mandatory too. I could cancel the dentist, but their teeth hurt already. That hardly seems right."

"The dentist is a once or twice thing, isn't it?" Karen asked. "That time will open up soon."

"You would think so, wouldn't you? But I've had that appointment a couple times already. They canceled it at the last minute both times. The last time they waited until I was walking in the door. When you pay with a Medicaid card, you're not even worth a phone call."

They sympathized but maintained that it was my responsibility to clear my schedule so I could get Tina to her visits. The implication was that I should quit work.

"When I went down to Agency B to interview, I went with a question. My question was 'Is this doable?' I laid out my circumstances. I am a single parent. I have to keep up my nursing skills by working a little. I was reassured that it was doable because I would be getting so much support. Where is that support?"

"You have a social worker who supports you."

"Maybe we need to define 'support.'"

"Maybe you need to tell us what you would consider support." Lesley, the new worker who was probably terrified by now, finally spoke up.

"I think this is a perfect example. I need someone who will fill in gaps, provide rides. No, wait! First of all, I need a worker who is on time for their appointments, both picking them up and dropping them off. Marie has missed tutoring twice because Pam didn't bring the kids back on time. Then I need someone who is willing to do, not just talk. If you have to spend an hour with the kids, why not make it an hour that is useful to me. All that continuing education I'm supposed to get…everything started at 8 A.M. The kids don't leave here until 8:15. Who do you think is going to baby-sit for two special needs kids for an hour that early in the morning? You could. Giving them breakfast and getting them out the door for school would involve you in their lives more than going to McDonald's does."

"You're right," she said.

"Great."

To pacify Karen, Lesley agreed to drive Tina to her visits "until something opens up" in my schedule. But it was over. We were done. I won. Getting Lesley, young but not immature, may have been the biggest win of all that day. But why did it have to be so hard?

I often say the kids are the easy part.

Then I remember Tina. She was not easy. She was a tornado either whirling through the house decorating it with "I love you" messages or screaming at me to "Fuck off." She was a seven-year-old. And she was a seventeen-year-old. She was never an eleven-year-old.

Her probation officer, the beautiful Joanne, had the same dilemma. She would see Tina and I sitting out in the waiting room, surrounded by surly teenagers with dyed black hair, glittering with body piercings, and want to respond to us as if the little darling had just arrived. She had to stop herself from cooing over Tina like I do over kids in the ER who need stitches. But Tina's crimes were probably the most serious in the waiting room. The six-foot boy with the pimply face may have a drunk and disorderly or a burglary charge, but Tina was the only one who hurt people. Joanne had to remind herself and keep her tone as serious as it would have been if Tina were older.

And she reminded Tina every week that the only reason she wasn't in The Youth Center was her age. She was ten when she went before the judge and eleven was the youngest age a child could be incarcerated. Tina had to walk the straight and narrow, the very straight and very narrow.

There was a certain amount of burden on me when it came to reporting on her behavior. She was never perfect. Who is? But what might get Stephen grounded, like hitting or pushing, could get her jailed. It was up to me.

She came very close late one cold November afternoon. We were walking out to the car after swimming at a local hotel that offered members use of a pool and exercise room.

It was an experiment and the kids knew it. We had a one-week pass and if things worked out, we would join, as I had when my own kids were younger. It meant a lot to me. I suppose, in part, I was trying to recreate the fun I'd had when Tony and Renee were young, splashing in the pool, soaking in the hot tub. But I also craved the time it gave me all to myself, watching Entertainment Tonight from a treadmill, while the kids splashed and soaked without me.

The exercise room faced the pool and was surrounded by glass so I was able to walk on the treadmill, watch TV and keep an eye on the kids at the same time. My foster parent friend Carol had asked if her thirteen-year-old daughter Eleanor could come too, so the four of us gave it a try. I had been clear about two things on the drive down to the Sheraton Tara:

Rule 1. They were not to run in and out of the exercise room ratting on each other. They were not to come in at all, unless someone was bleeding or drowning. But since I could see everything anyway, and I would know if anyone was bleeding or drowning, really there was no reason to come in at all. They agreed.

Rule 2. If Eleanor was to come along, she had to play with both kids, not play with one and ignore the other, stirring up hurt feelings. She agreed.

Kids have such short memories. That's all I can figure. The door to the exercise room opened so many times there was humidity running down the walls from the pool.

"They won't play with me!"

"Tina splashed me!"

"Stephen keeps bothering us!"

It was a dismal failure and they heard about my disappointment all the way out to the car.

"So are we going to join?" Tina asked as if she hadn't heard a word I said.

"No!" I bellowed just as I was unlocking the car doors so we could all get in and stop shivering. Tina was poised to enter the car, but turned when I yelled and darted for a nearby patch of grass instead, plopping down cross-legged with a scowl on her face.

I held the car door open. "Get in," I ordered. She didn't budge.

"Fine," I said, and the rest of us got in. I waited a minute for her to respond. When she didn't, I pulled out of the parking space.

My heart was pounding. I expected her to panic at the thought of me leaving without her and run to catch up. But she didn't move. I had pulled the car out into a line of cars that were waiting for me to move. I had to keep driving, and found myself pulling out onto the highway all the while looking around for another alternative. Stephen started to whimper in the back seat and Eleanor said, "You can't do this. It's child abuse."

"I'm going back. I just want to scare her a little."

I'm screwed, I thought to myself when I pulled back into the parking lot and Tina wasn't on the patch of grass anymore. It was getting dark as I took the same parking spot and got out of the car to look around.

"Stay where you are, " I said to the other two. "I'm going to check inside." She wasn't there either.

I was at the front desk asking if anyone had seen her when Steve and Eleanor ran in breathless with the information that they had spotted her. She was under a car hiding from me.

I went out, reached under the car and dragged her out by the arm. She was screaming and hitting and scratching with all her might. We were on the ground together, me straddling her, trying to prevent her rolling back under the car. I had her arms pinned to the ground so she couldn't get to me to draw blood when she suddenly stopped screaming just long enough to spit in my eye.

My hand flew at her face. I came so-o-o-o close to slapping her. I stopped just in time to cover her mouth with my hand so she couldn't spit again, but I still wanted desperately to hit her. In all my years as a nurse, taking care of angry patients, alcoholics and psych patients, no one had ever spit on me before. I had no idea how it felt. I had no idea how angry I could get. Later that night I lay awake fantasizing about strangling her. It wasn't the initial tantrum or the hour and three quarters it took to get her in the car. It was the saliva dripping down my face that enraged me.

After trying unsuccessfully to get Tina into the car, I went back in the hotel and called the Agency B Emergency number. The person on call said, "Who are you supposed to call for emergencies?"

I said, "You."

She said, "Don't you have any friends you could call?"

I finally called Eleanor's parents, Carol and Chris. They are both tall people, Chris is probably six and a half feet tall and burly. He only said, "Get in the car" once and she did.

When we got home and she was safely inside, so I knew I wasn't going to go through the whole thing all over again, I sent her to her room, loudly. She responded with some obscenity or another but she went. I didn't care as long as I didn't have to look at her again for the rest of the evening, maybe for the rest of my life, but for now just the evening would do.

I knew that by law I had to feed her so I called up the stairs when our pathetic dinner was ready. My plan had been to pick up something on the drive home, as we were short on groceries, but in all of the excitement I forget.

"Supper's ready, Tina," I called.

"Go fuck yourself!" she called back as I fully expected.

Hours later, I heard her pacing around in her room and I knew that she had to be starving as she hadn't eaten since lunch. I brought her up a plate of food. Four slices of whole wheat bread and a glass of water. We had had the same thing plus cheese slices between the bread. Cheese sandwiches. Bread and water. Not much difference, but enough to get me reprimanded by Agency B. It is against policy to feed kids bread and water. It would have been okay not to feed her at all, since I had offered and she refused, but it is not okay to feed bread and water.

The funny thing is Tina thanked me for the bread and water that night and the next day during her profuse apology. She said she was so hungry it was the best thing she ever tasted.

"I used to think I hated wheat bread," she said. "Now I love it."

In retrospect I wish I had handled the whole thing differently. I wish I had marched the other two kids back into the hotel restaurant and ordered dinner. I should have calmly informed her that we were eating and she could join us when she was ready. I should have just waited her out.

Others said I should have called the police. The whole thing was a probation violation. I could have done it after the fact but I didn't. I decided to give her one more chance.

Christmas season came and went. My daughter Renee joined a friend's family for the holidays instead of coming home because she didn't think it would be "restful" enough at our house. Maybe it was more restful with her friend, but she missed out on one of those magical Christmas moments that can't be planned and will stay in all of our memories forever.

One unseasonably warm evening we decided to take advantage of the weather and hang Christmas lights outside. We hung what we had, but it was so beautiful out it seemed a shame to stop. So we zipped over to the Rite Aid and bought a dozen more strings of lights. There was no method to our madness, and no art in the results, but by the time we were done the house was ablaze with blinking lights and night had turned into day on our front sidewalk. Just as we stood back to admire our handiwork, the CD player came to "Little Saint Nick," one of the few Christmas songs that lends itself to wild dancing. The Muppets have an especially fine version of it on their album with John Denver.

We turned up the volume and Steve, Tina, Marie and I danced our hearts out, but the song was over too soon. We replayed it a few times, and then wanting to dance some more, replaced the Christmas music with The Backstreet Boys. By this time the neighbors were peeking out their windows and a few joined us. It was so silly and so much fun; it was hard to finally call it a night. I try to find that moment right before someone gets overtired and forces a bad ending. We danced up the steps and into the house at long last. For the rest of the Christmas season, Tina begged for a repeat every chance she got.

"It's twenty degrees out there, Tina."

"I don't care."

I wondered how it compared to "partying with teenagers in a motel room" for Tina. For a kid who had done things like that, she never appeared to be especially jaded. She still knew how to be a little kid and just have a good time.

My son Tony spent Christmas with us even if Renee didn't and it was fine. We went to the Nutcracker as well as The Magic of Christmas. Steve and Tina were difficult, just because they were rowdy, noisy kids but they weren't really bad.

It was a short time after Christmas that Tina blew her second chance. It wasn't a huge incident. It was nothing like the episode in the parking lot. It was just a fight with Marie. Marie told her to clean up the mess she made in the front hall when she came in with snowy boots on. Instead, Tina walked over to the couch and sat down in defiance. When Marie tried to force the issue, Tina kicked her in the shins.

I sent Tina to her room, but I sent Marie as well as it was not her place to be bossing Tina around for the umpteenth time. I put in a call to Lesley and we talked it through. It had been said too many times that Tina could not do anything that could be considered assault. She had been warned that her probation was dependent on her continued lack of criminal offenses. It was time to make good on the threat, to let Tina learn what the threat actually was by experiencing it.

I called Joanne, the probation officer, and she met us at the Youth Center. It was a Thursday. Little Tina would literally be a prisoner until Sunday. I felt bad. I would have felt better if it was a bigger incident. But it wasn't exactly an isolated incident either. I thought about the problems she continued to cause at home and at school. She called a classmate a nigger, which got her sentenced to the entire *Roots* series. (She ended up quite sorry and wrote a letter to the boy saying so.) And she pulled sneaky little numbers on me just to show how smart she was, like the incident with the skin cream.

I had taken Tina from doctor to doctor trying to solve the problem of her remarkably dry skin. They prescribed various skin creams, and I kept a chart showing which one was used and what effect it had on her rashy, itchy skin. My only mistake was giving Tina the medicine and having her smear it on after her shower. After months of wasted time and money, I discovered that she had never even broken the seal on the first medicine.

"You never used any of this, did you?" I asked when I confronted her.

Her usual cackle erupted from deep in her throat and she dropped to the floor laughing. She had been waiting and waiting for that moment. It was the ultimate practical joke in her eyes.

She could be hard to like.

As I drove away from the Youth Center, guilt-ridden, I passed the spot where I met Tina in the first place, in a parking lot behind the Kidspeace offices. I thought about that day, what I expected and what I got. She was such an odd child, odd looking and odd acting.

Sometimes an idea bursts into consciousness like a light bulb turning on, but this time was more like a chick pecking its way out of an egg. Odd looking and odd acting, I thought again.

An FLK.

That's medical for Funny Looking Kid, like SOB is medical for Short of Breath. I hadn't heard it used in a while, but in nurses' training they talked about how babies with one thing wrong at birth usually have three, so being an FLK is ominous. If things are scrambled on the outside, they're probably scrambled on the inside. Like Down's Syndrome for example. The face is not the only problem. There is also the mental retardation and the heart disease.

I had met the rest of Tina's family by now. She wasn't like them. They were normal looking, even attractive. The older girls had gotten in some trouble as teenagers, one even being a teen mother, but nothing like Tina.

Syndrome. Down's Syndrome. Trisomey 13 Syndrome. I knew there were actually hundreds, maybe thousands of syndromes, most of them rare, many of them incompatible with life. There were books in medical libraries with page after page of syndromes. Oh, damn, I thought, I've got to go to the library.

I didn't expect to do this again in my life. When my son, Tony, was diagnosed as autistic I combed libraries and read everything in sight about autism or anything like it. Some things I read rang true and I would use the advice offered. Other things just didn't sit right and I put the book aside knowing the information wasn't going to be useful. I couldn't explain it any better than that. My gut lead me down the right path in my research. Tony is no longer autistic.

My heart was pounding as I walked into the Medical Center Library the next day. My gut said I was on the right path again.

I knew the books would be horrifying. Every page with a syndrome, every syndrome with a picture or two of the victims. It is amazing the number of things that can go wrong in human conception. Each page was worse than the one before, but most of the pictures were of infants or dead fetuses. These children either died or had reconstructive surgery so the general public didn't even know the extent of the possibilities. I didn't want to know myself.

I finished one entire volume without seeing anything that vaguely resembled Tina. I set it aside and started the next, discouraged and slightly nauseated. I flipped through pages, looking quickly, then moving on. It was like driving by a car accident. I wanted to look. I didn't want to look.

Then I turned a page and there was Tina. I was as shocked by that picture as all of the rest so I kept on turning pages. Then I stopped and took a deep breath. Maybe it was my imagination. I turned back and looked again. There was a boy, standing in his underwear, with the year 1976 in small print below it. But it was Tina. The flat nose, the bug eyes, no neck, short stature. They were all there. There were even things about her I had noticed only in passing, but not given much thought to, like the way she held her arms away from her body like an over muscled body builder. The child in the photo did the same.

I quickly read the description of Hurler-Scheie Syndrome or Mucopolysaccharidosis I. Much of what I read was Greek to me, even as an RN, because the text was written for geneticists and steeped in terms only they would understand. But I understood the list headed Abnormalities. Under it was mild mental deficiency, short stature with especially short neck, coarse facial features with low nasal bridge and prominent lips, thick skin, moderate joint limitations and Hepatosplenomegaly. That means enlarged liver and spleen, hence the potbelly.

Under Natural History was "Onset of symptoms usually between 3 and 8 years with survival into the 20s common. Onset of corneal clouding, joint limitations, cardiac valvular abnormalities and hearing impairment frequently develop by the early to mid teens."

Tina had a syndrome all right and it was fatal.

CHAPTER 9

✦ ✦ ✦

What Do You Think "Partying" Means?

Tina was maybe a little bit contrite when she got back from The Youth Center. Measured on a one to ten scale, she was probably a one whereas before she was a zero. At first she tried to convince us it was "cool," but later she admitted she had cried herself to sleep at night. Some of the girls thought she was cute, but others threatened her. I hoped her behavior would improve, but I had a whole different slant on it now. I wondered how you change behavior that is biological in origin and how you treat it. Is it still punishable?

Xerox copies of the pages I had found in the medical library were in the mail to Tina's pediatrician, psychiatrist, social worker and probation officer by the time I picked her up from The Youth Center. During the next week they called, one by one, to say, "Oh my god!" Her psychiatrist set up an appointment for her with a geneticist. Her DHS worker cried.

Lillian's call took me by surprise because it came the next Saturday. Apparently she went in to the office on her day off to catch up on paperwork and found my packet of information. It hit her hard.

For some inexplicable reason she adored Tina and the feeling was mutual. The only time I saw them together, when Lillian came out for a visit, Tina spent the whole time on Lillian's lap saying, "I wish you were my mother." It seemed odd to me, as Tina also loved her real mother, crying for her at night, begging to call or visit her during the day. She knew Lillian was the one who took her away from her mother and planned to keep her away, but she still snuggled and kissed Lillian's cheek like a long lost grandmother. Tina didn't seem to think things through.

Lillian had never tried to conceal the hostility she felt for Tina's mother when she spoke to me. She would tell of Tina's mother crying in her office about how hard it was to get to all the appointments that were made for her, as well as hold down a full time job, as well as be a good mother to the four other children in her home. Lillian admitted to me that she had piled on these requirements to assure her failure to comply. I expressed sympathy once and Lillian said, "Oh, boo hoo, must be nice letting the state raise your kid."

"But it wasn't her choice." I reminded her.

"I've lived in this town for a long time," she told me. "I know this family and they are scum. If she wanted her kid back she'd make it to her appointments and stop crying about it."

I wondered if I'd want Tina back, after all she'd put her family through, but I didn't say it. Mom did find a ride all the way to Portland when Tina graduated from white belt to gold in karate. And she met us for dinner at Blimpie's a few times. I got the impression she cared a great deal about Tina, but she was tired, profoundly tired. She talked to me about getting up in the morning and finding Tina missing, about searching for her, and about fearing Tina would be taken away if she called the police and said she'd lost her again.

When I mentioned that to Lillian, the DHS worker, she said, "She didn't look for her until she was gone four days." I didn't know whom to believe. And what I believed was irrelevant anyway.

I didn't owe Tina's mother an apology, but I certainly thought the state did. Tina's behavior was not the result of abuse. In my research on the Internet I had found pitifully little on the rare condition Tina was afflicted with, but I did read one case study of a patient whose presenting symptom was a behavior problem. I mentioned that when Lillian called that Saturday, since it wasn't in my original packet. There was silence on the other end of the phone. She was willing to talk about what this all meant to Tina, but not to her family. I didn't push it. I thought there was plenty of time for that, after the geneticist verified her diagnosis.

What Do You Think "Partying" Means?

✦ ✦ ✦

One night, two weeks after Tina got home, I put the two little ones to bed and went back downstairs. The minute I hit the bottom stair I realized I had missed an opportunity to give Tina some positive reinforcement. She had taken some correction from me earlier in the day with more maturity than usual and I didn't want her to think it had gone unnoticed. So I went back up the stairs.

"Tina," I said standing in her dark room, "I wanted to tell you what a great job you did...Tina?"

My eyes were adjusting to the light and I realized she wasn't in bed. "Tina?"

I thought she might be hiding in the closet, kidder that she was, "Tina!"

She was not in her room. I checked the bathroom, then Marie's room and the TV room. I walked into Stephen's room.

"Have you seen Tina?" I asked. He looked at me over the edge of his blanket, wide-eyed.

"Stephen," I insisted, "Do you know where Tina is?"

He pointed towards the foot end of his bed. There, between his knees and the wall, was a lump under the blanket.

"GET OUT!" I bellowed.

She didn't move.

"GET OUT!" I yelled louder if that is possible.

When she still didn't move, I reached under the blankets, grabbed her by an arm and a leg and pulled her out depositing her on the floor with a clunk. She stayed in knee/chest position as if frozen.

"Go to your room!"

I was wasting my breath. After yet another order was ignored, I picked her up by the same two extremities and carried her to her room dropping her on the floor again. I made no effort to do it gently. I was furious. I slammed her door so hard it shook the house.

I was shaking and so was my voice when I went back into Stephen's room. Before I could even ask, he answered, "She's been doing that every night."

"For how long?"

"A long time."

"Doing what?"

"Getting into my bed."

"Then what?"

"I don't understand," he started to whimper.

"What was she doing under your covers?" I bellowed.

"Nothing." he said, but his eyes said everything. It was a foster parent's nightmare. A foster child had been molested in my home. How could I have let it happen?

I couldn't understand how Tina could have gone undetected. I was directly below her watching TV or working on the computer in the evenings. The house was so old and creaky everyone knew every time someone else went to the bathroom. I found out later Tina used my footsteps to disguise hers. She slipped into Stephen's room as I walked downstairs, immediately after our sweet hug and kiss goodnight time. Then she slipped back into her room when Marie started getting ready for bed and was walking back and forth between her room and the bathroom. And extra set of footsteps then would go unnoticed. I remembered that a few weeks earlier, Steve had requested that the hall light be out after he went to bed. That way no one could see in, if they happened to be in the hall. That must have been when it began. It was very well thought out, by both of them.

I called the DHS emergency line with Tina screaming obscenities and threats in the background. I wanted to get her out that night. I kept picturing Tony at Steve's age and wondering what I would be doing to her if it was him who was molested. How sad for Stephen that my action was less than that. The person on call at DHS happened to be familiar with Tina's case.

"Wasn't there an alarm on the door?" he asked.

"No."

"Why the hell not? She shouldn't have even been in a home with a younger child with her history." he said as if I was to blame, which I certainly felt I was.

"I was specifically told she did not have a history of sexual abuse."

"What do you think she was doing in a motel room full of teenagers? What did you think 'partying' meant?"

My biggest concern was in getting through that night. She was already up there threatening to kill someone and with the history I did know; I could see it happening. The worker said there was nothing he could do about the situation, and that my only options were to take her to an Emergency Room or get through the night as best we could.

I knew the Emergency Room scenario too well to view that as an option. I'd seen it a hundred times. We would wait for hours, first in the waiting room, then in an exam room and then for a crisis worker. Stephen and Marie would be left home alone. I could be charged with desertion if I left Tina in the ER alone, or with a licensing violation if I left the other two. Then in the morning we would be sent home to do the same thing we would have done if we hadn't spent the night in the Emergency Room but now with an even more severe sleep deprivation going for us. I said we would stay home, but I was locking her in her room.

"That's against the law," he told me.

"So I should stay awake and guard her door, or just take my chances?"

"I don't know, but you can't lock her door."

"What would you do?"

He was getting annoyed. "Just don't tell me about it."

In the morning Tina quietly packed her things. By noon she was back at The Youth Center.

Sometime later, a DHS worker came by to pick up her things, saying that Tina was going to another foster home. I later learned that foster care arrangement was canceled and she was sent to an even more restricted place for girls a few hours north of here. She must have done something. I called her DHS worker to remind her of Tina's appointment with the geneticist, but she had me cancel it. Tina wouldn't be permitted to leave the facility for quite some time.

Soon after, the geneticist, the only one in the state, left his practice. The closest one now is two hours south. So Tina is four hours away from a definitive diagnosis. Maybe it doesn't matter anyway. There is no treatment and she still has to be restrained from hurting other people somehow. I could call and ask for an update, but I'm not on the list of people they are allowed to tell anymore. It's none of my business. I still wonder if her mother knows.

Tina was only with us for four months though it seemed like a lot longer. Her leaving didn't convince Marie to stay as she left only a few weeks later. The departures are always so emotional for me. So much like failures.

There is one picture of Tina on the mantelpiece. She has one arm around Steve and the other around a giant Halloween scarecrow in our front yard. She and Steve have their heads tilted towards each other and big grins on their faces...big conspiratorial grins.

Brian

I was a triage nurse when a four-year-old girl was brought to the ER after "falling down the stairs." The only marks left on her were two black eyes. Mom wanted to be sure she didn't have a head injury, as she was behaving strangely.

The child looked me right in the eye, but refused to even gesture in response to questions about how she got hurt. Grandma stood in the background wiping tears from her eyes, once stepping into the restroom to sob for a moment.

It was the first time I felt certain I had un-covered child abuse. I expected the doctor to come looking for me to file a report.

Instead, the child was discharged with a clean bill of health in twelve minutes.

"You didn't think that was suspicious?" I asked the doctor.

"Yes, but I know the mother. She wouldn't have hit her child."

As a mandatory reporter myself, I went ahead and called the child abuse hotline. A week later I was summoned to the Medical Director's office.

"Do you know who you were dealing with?" he asked me, incredulous. He then proceeded to tell me of the family's high standing in the com-munity.

"Would you have filed a report if you didn't know the mother," I asked, "if she was paying with a Medicaid card?"

"Probably," he answered.

CHAPTER 10

✦ ✦ ✦

Syrup of Ipecac

It was about this time, I found myself seriously addicted to Freecell. It's a computer game, similar to Solitaire, but with a better chance of winning. I discovered it in the weeks between Marie's leaving and Brian's coming. I still use it to block intrusive thoughts like, "What the hell have I gotten myself into?"

I was staring at the monitor, one day, developing repetitive motion injuries, when I realized what the attraction was. In Freecell, there is so much time spent hopeful. The sense of failure is brief and with a click of the mouse it's over. New game, click, hope again. Nothing like life. Nothing like foster care.

I couldn't grab some new kid immediately after the last one left and feel hopeful again. I needed recovery time. I needed time to process and learn from the last experience. The remaining family needed to regroup. There was secret crying to do and, after that, rooms to clean and clothes to pack. But there were also bills to pay.

I was just gathering my strength to go down to Ann's office and peruse the referral stack again when she called with a boy she said was right up my alley.

"Have you ever heard of Munchausen by Proxy Abuse?" she asked me.

"Sure," I answered. Not only had I heard of it, described in simplest terms as medical child abuse, but I had studied it. Not for a class or anything. I hadn't officially been in school for a decade, but I became interested in Munchausen by Proxy Syndrome from a Geraldo TV program and went on to read several books on the subject.

I still remember my introduction to MBP. I was working in the ER, as usual, and went out to the waiting room to call another patient back. The TV was on and I got there just in time to hear a TV talk show "expert" say that nine out of ten female serial killers are health care professionals. I gasped! Part of me wanted to run over and snap the TV off, but another part, curiosity, made me stand and watch. I waited until I heard the name of the book being pushed and scribbled it down on a piece of paper. Then I called the patient back for treatment.

The book, *From Cradle to Grave,* was about a nurse's aid named Marybeth Tinnings, who suffocated all eight of her children one by one, then claimed to have found each one of them dead in a crib. The medical and legal establishment at the time accepted that they had all inherited some defect that lead to SIDS. She was finally caught when an adopted child died exactly the same way as her natural children. She did it for the attention of first, being the devoted mother of a sick child; then, being the courageous, grieving mother of a dead child. She was addicted to that attention. It was her identity and without it, she felt she was nothing. The parent is said to have Munchausen by Proxy Syndrome. The child suffers Munchausen by Proxy Abuse.

The name has to do with the fact that it is an offshoot of Munchausen Syndrome, wherein a person gets the attention they seek by making themselves sick. When it is another they make sick, it is "by proxy."

"I just got a call," Ann continued. "There is a fourteen year old boy in Maine Med…"

"Wait a minute," I interrupted. "How is that possible? Wouldn't a fourteen year old know if his mother was holding a pillow over his face?" My reading had only uncovered cases in which the children were under five and the mechanism of injury was usually suffocation.

"I don't know the details," Ann went on. "The DHS worker was really evasive. Secretive even. She only asked if we had a foster parent with a medical background, one who lives near the hospital and one who could keep a child for a very long time. They need to see what happens to his health when he is away from his mother. And I suppose there is the possibility he will get sick again and they want a foster parent who would know what to do."

"You've got me," I said, tickled that my abilities as a nurse/parent had finally been recognized. "What do I do next?"

How could I say no to something that sounded so intriguing? Plus I knew instinctively that I would be considered a hero if this child grew and flourished in my care, as he likely would just by virtue of no longer being made sick. If he didn't, and it was determined that he actually was a sick child, I would be his mother's hero for proving her innocence. My bruised ego was going to love this case. Or so I thought.

That hero fantasy of mine provides strong motivation, which may explain some of my original fascination with MBP syndrome. I understand the motivation. I just can't conceive of acting on it in such a heartless manner.

Ann said the DHS worker would call me herself with the details, treating Ann as the unnecessary middleman. All information would be shared on a "need to know" basis. There was a criminal case to prosecute here. Leaking of information could taint that case. I said I understood and waited anxiously for the call.

When Janet did call there was only one of the original three requirements that she repeated. She didn't mention my being a nurse or living near the hospital. She just said, "You have to be committed to keep this child for a very long time."

"I do long term," I told her, thinking that would satisfy her.

"No. I mean really long. Like until he grows up."

"That's my goal with every child. Isn't that what 'long term' means?"

"Okay, just so we understand each other." She then dropped her volume a notch and continued. "His name is Brian. He is fourteen. He has spent his whole life believing that he has a rare congenital disease and that his brother died of it."

"She killed his brother?"

"I can't say."

"Was it Muscular Dystrophy, the thing he thought he had?"

"No, but you're close. He was in the ICU. He was being let go." She paused. "I mean it was like his last day of life, when some doctor looked at him and said 'this doesn't look like a neurological coma. It looks like a drug overdose.' He gave two medicines to undo the effects of other medicines…"

"Narcan and Romazicon." I told her, "One reverses narcotics and the other reverses benzodiazipines."

"Right. Well, he woke up. Then they barred the mother from the hospital and he just kept improving. Now he's going to physical therapy to get his strength back. He probably won't be strong enough to go to school for a month or more. But he needs to live with someone with a medical background…"

"In case he relapses, if he really is sick?" I asked.

"Oh, no, that's pretty well proven. They did a muscle biopsy and it came back negative. But he might have complications just from being an invalid for so long. You know he hasn't eaten normally for months. He had a feeding tube."

I gasped. I was starting to get the picture.

"He had one of those permanent IVs, implanted under the skin, you know, for medicine." I could hear her getting choked up too on the other end of the phone.

"A Hickman catheter?"

"Yeah. He had a tube in his bladder too. He hasn't even taken a leak on his own."

"Oh, my Lord!"

"He was a Do Not Resuscitate, a DNR," she said, obviously incredulous herself. "His burial arrangements were made."

"That makes me want to cry," I said. "That doctor saved his life. Do you know who it was?"

I knew many of the doctors at the Maine Medical Center. I'd worked in that ICU for six years, though it was about that many years ago. I wondered if I would know the person. Already I wanted to thank him.

"I don't. I could find out. This whole case is so emotional to me. To everyone. Some of the nurses are very angry."

"At the mom."

"No, at me. At the doctor who uncovered it. They don't believe she did it. They got to be friends with her."

"That's classic," I said. "That's what MBP mothers do. They present themselves as so wonderful that no one would ever doubt them."

"Yeah, well I got to be the one to tell Brian that his wonderful mom wasn't so wonderful after all."

"How did he take it?"

"Like I was telling him his lunch tray was going to be late. He didn't show one flicker of emotion."

"Do you think someone else already told him?"

"It sure seemed that way, though everyone denies it. He hadn't seen his mother in four days though and didn't ask anyone where she was either. That was a puzzle. And when I said he wouldn't be seeing her at all he asked if he could still see his step dad. That's all. He didn't ask how we knew she did it. He didn't ask what would happen to her or to him. Nothing. He's a very passive kid. I told him he would be going to a foster home and he asked if he could go to one with a dog."

"Damn."

"No dog?"

"No. Tell him we're getting one."

"Are you?"

"We are now."

Steve and I walked onto the Barbara Bush Wing of the Maine Medical Center the next afternoon and stopped at the nurse's station as I'd been instructed. The half a dozen people at the desk looked up or turned around to check us out. I had to show picture ID and then was escorted in to meet Brian by a hospital social worker.

He looked like a gray running-suit with a head on it. His head, square in shape, was pretty cute, with big brown eyes and thick brown hair. But there didn't appear to be a body in that running-suit except for the pale thin fingers that poked out of the sleeves. He smiled when introduced to us. It wasn't a big warm smile, but it wasn't an insincere smile either. It was a gracious smile. He reached up and shook my hand at the same time. When did this child have time to learn manners, I asked myself.

The social worker left us alone and Steve and I proceeded to tell Brian about the family he would be joining. He listened. He laughed at Steve's description of his messy room. Brian said he was a slob too so they'd get along fine. I threw in something like, "I know you've been through a lot," and he shrugged as if to say it was nothing much really.

Then he said, "Oh, guess what? I walked by myself today in Physical Therapy. Wanna see?"

"Sure," I said.

"We can go for a walk if you want to. I'll introduce you to the nurses here."

"Should I get a wheelchair in case you get tired?"

"I won't," he answered confidently and he didn't. We walked around two different nurse's stations and into the big playroom finding friends of his. True to his word, he introduced us to everyone. Some of them

87

looked as nonplused as I was by his adult behavior. Some were just shocked to see him walking. Everyone got tears in their eyes.

"I'm leaving in two days," he told me. "Will you pick me up?"

"I will be happy to."

"When can I start school?"

"They tell me you won't be ready physically for about a month."

"It won't take that long," he said. "How about next week?"

And so it was. Brian moved in on a Saturday, and started school the second Monday after. We had nine days to get to know each other before his focus shifted from home and family to friends at school. They were a delightful nine days. Brian was delightful.

When Stephen was home the boys jumped on the trampoline or played video games. There was some competition, but mostly the friendly sort. Brian had it all over Stephen in cleverness. But Stephen could turn a somersault on the trampoline. He had to give Brian lessons.

When Stephen was at school, Brian and I climbed Douglas Mountain, walked along the beach and talked. Most of our conversations were light. He had lots of stories of Little League games and fishing with his grandfather. I told him all about my own kids, Renee and Tony, about living in New Mexico and being a nurse and a foster mother. We got along as if we'd known each other forever, but I reminded myself that he was used to keeping company mostly with grown-ups, mostly with his mom. I probably reminded him of her.

On his third day with us, he was keeping me company in the kitchen while I cooked, and I made a comment about this being a difficult time for him. He answered, "Not really."

I must have looked quizzically at him because he added, "It's sort of like I really did die in the hospital, but I got reincarnated. This is my new life. I miss everybody, but I sure like being healthy."

"What a great way to think of it," I said. "Would you take the old way back again if you could, knowing you'd be a sick kid?"

He thought about it and said no. He really liked being well.

"I guess that was a silly question, wasn't it?" I added. "With the old way, you weren't just sick. You were dying. Nobody would choose to go back to that."

He looked at me like I was exaggerating. "I wasn't dying," he said. "I've had relapses before. I would have been okay."

I thought it was time to change the subject, so I tried to do that with supper as the new topic. He still looked agitated.

"She didn't do it," he said bluntly. "I knew every pill I ever took. I was there for every conversation with the doctors. I would have known."

It was too soon for me to have an opinion or for him to hear it. So I kept digging through the cupboards for the right pan. There was an awkward silence.

"I did notice one thing," he said finally, almost under his breath.

"Yeah?" I tried to be casual.

"Once I snuck over to my neighbor's house and ate a cheeseburger. It was the only time I didn't throw up."

"Hmmm." I turned and looked at him sitting at the kitchen table. It was clear he was trying to think this one through.

"But I guess you can't make someone throw up," he said suddenly, happy with that conclusion.

"Sure you can," I answered, "Syrup of Ipecac."

"What?"

"Syrup of Ipecac. You give it to kids who have taken poison or pills or something and you want them to throw it right back up."

"That stuff in the little brown bottle?" he asked.

I nodded. His brows furrowed and the corners of his mouth turned down.

I was so relieved his DHS worker as well as the detective on the case were visiting later in the week. I desperately needed guidance on what to do with that kind of information. I knew there was great concern about "the case." Of course I was concerned about it too because Brian's future depended on it. But I was also concerned with "the kid." What did he need to hear? Was reassurance more important than facing reality? And what should I expect from him? It seemed logical that depression would set in at some point. Maybe anger. Maybe even faked illness as illness was all he ever knew and that might make his mother seem less guilty. What would I do if I caught him sneaking phone calls to his mother? That seemed like another real possibility. I wanted to proceed carefully to protect him as well as his case.

Janet came out on Wednesday morning with his guardian *ad litem*. All foster kids have a guardian *ad litem* (GAL). They are meant to serve as the child's voice in court. They are to get to know the child well enough to speak for him by frequent visits and phone calls. Some are CASA volunteers. Some are volunteer lawyers.

I was glad they came together so I could get some alone time with Janet while Brian was with his guardian *ad litem*. There was so much to discuss.

For one thing Brian had inadvertently told his step dad what school he would be attending on his supervised visit. This was a serious problem.

"Maybe we should send him to the other middle school across town." I suggested. I was a little panicky that the solution might be moving him to a different foster home. My research on the Internet indicated that MBP victims are usually placed in foster homes out of state, as kidnapping is a very real risk. MBP parents are notorious for slipping out from under accusations by moving to another state. Brian's mother had already done that three times. This would be the first time she had to kidnap him to do it because this was the first time he was taken away. But she had been detected and accused before, then disappeared with the help of her wealthy parents. I learned this part of the story after Brian moved in, and I was frightened for him.

"I don't think changing schools would help," Janet said. "There is only one other school he could go to and she'd find him there if she wanted to. I think the key is to watch him. Are you able to drive him to school and pick him up every day?"

"Of course," If it was a hardship I would deal with that on my own.

"I've had kids on my caseload who were kidnap risks before. It's important that the school is aware of it and you develop a code for asking about him. If the caller doesn't use the code, they know not to give out any information."

"Okay."

"And I would suggest you drive around the school and look for his mother's car a few minutes before school is out. I have a feeling he would not need to be coaxed to get in with her."

"I don't know what to look for."

"Laurie, the detective, knows the makes and license numbers of both of their cars. I'll call her and have her bring them out to you Thursday."

"Okay."

Finally we got to talk about the conversation I had had with Brian about the vomiting and Janet was very clear. She told me to direct him to bring those concerns to his psychiatrist or to her.

"Be very careful not to give him any information he doesn't already have. Like the Syrup of Ipecac. If he testifies that he thinks his mother gave him Syrup of Ipecac, the defense lawyer is sure to ask where he got that idea. If he says 'My foster mother told me' his whole testimony is tainted as possibly being influenced by you."

It made sense. I vowed to be more cautious in the future.

When Laurie, the detective, came out for a visit a few days later, we had to get Brian off the trampoline to accomplish anything. Steve was home from school by then and the two of them were playing "popcorn." Laurie got tears in her eyes when she saw how much fun Brian was having.

"The last time I saw him, he was a rag doll," she whispered. "The nurse scooped him up in her arms and put him in the wheelchair like he didn't weigh a thing. Then she had to pick each arm up and put it on the armrest. He couldn't speak above a whisper."

"Wow."

"I can't believe how different he looks. Has he gained weight?"

"A few pounds. He's only been here a week."

"Is he eating?"

"Plenty."

"No nausea?"

"None."

"Sleeping?"

"Soundly."

"No bizarre behavior?"

"Like what?"

"His mother said he was 'violent and abusive' toward her. She's trying to say she gave him all those drugs because of behavior problems that were the result of that disease, that MELOS, he supposedly had."

MELOS is so rare that I had to look it up on the Internet to find out what it was. All I learned looking it up was that it led to frequent strokes.

"But he's proven not to have it. How can she still be saying he had behavior problems because of it?"

"She says the biopsy is wrong. She's sure he's going to have a relapse any day. Her lawyer calls about it constantly."

"Well, he's anything but violent. Bizarrely passive sometimes. Except with Stephen. Watch him play this game. He's determined to win, but weight wins on a trampoline, so he's trying to outsmart him."

We stood and watched for a while. They were hilarious, taking turns being the one curled up in a ball in the middle of the trampoline while the other tried to bounce him as high as he could. Brian would always end up bouncing so high he lost control and lost the game. Steve, 4 years younger, had 40 pounds on him.

"How do you mean he's passive?"

"So far he hasn't done one thing for himself. I'm trying to ease him gently into the real world, but he expects everything done for him. He expected me to wash his face for him."

"What? God, his mother babied him!"

"I guess if you're laying in a bed being fed through a tube, it makes sense that your mother washes your face. But when we've been hiking all day, I think he can wash his own face. I showed him how. He didn't know. But I don't think he's doing it. He's getting a little pimply."

"Once school starts, he'll get motivated."

"I hope so."

Laurie did remember to bring the license numbers and descriptions of his parent's cars. She reiterated that it was important that I be on the lookout for them.

"What do I do if I see them?"

"Call me. Call Janet."

"What if, God forbid, he goes with her?"

"Call the state police immediately. Have a description of the car and Brian's clothes. Call Janet and me too, but first get the state police involved. They're bound to get on the Turnpike at some point."

For this, I was willing to stop working Fridays.

Laurie wrenched Brian off the trampoline and they visited briefly. Then we all said good-bye. Brian didn't think much of any of the people assigned to his case. When I pointed that out he said, "Would you like people who were trying to put your mother in jail?"

"I guess not," I answered.

CHAPTER 11

✦ ✦ ✦

An Honest Mistake

Brian's real father had been out of the picture for years and his mother's husband, Rick, was Dad to him. The day I met Brian in the hospital, he told me that he thought Rick was his real dad until he heard a doctor say otherwise.

"When was that?" I asked, hoping it was an old wound.

"Yesterday."

Later, when we were hiking and shopping during our first week together, he mentioned an adoption ceremony that was canceled at the last minute because Rick "got a job in another state" and they had to move on the day it was to happen. I filed that story in the back of my mind for two reasons. For one thing, the quick move from state to state fit the Munchausen by Proxy pattern. For another, it negated a shocking story Brian had told me of hearing from a stranger that his father wasn't his father. It seemed clear Brian had lied to me on that first day. And the only purpose I could see was to arouse sympathy.

Brian had a supervised visit with Rick the Friday after he moved in with me. I took him downtown to Agency B for the meeting. We parked about a block away and walked by a dozen or more parked cars getting there. Just inside the front door of the building was a coffee vendor. We were going to take the elevator up four floors, when Brian looked at a gentleman waiting at the cart for his coffee and said, "Hi Dad!"

It was an awkward moment. They didn't hug, but they smiled, Brian bigger than Rick. Rick looked nervously at me and then Brian thought to introduce us.

"How do you like my new fleece?" Brian asked, turning around to show off his red hooded jacket.

"Very nice."

Then the counter person interrupted. "Your coffee, sir," she said.

Rick turned around and quickly paid for two cups of coffee. "I'll see you upstairs," he said, and walked back out the door of the building. Brian and I got on the elevator.

"Your dad seems nice," I said.

"I wonder who the other coffee was for," he said.

"Me, too."

My heart was pounding as I walked back out of the building to kill the hour while they visited. I knew she was out there, but I wanted to see for myself. As it turned out we had walked right by her, sitting on the passenger side of one of the two cars I'd been told to watch out for.

I walked around the block and went in the back door of the building and back upstairs. I was breathless when I asked the secretary if she could call into the room where the meeting was going on and get Lesley on the phone.

"His mother is sitting in a car in front of the building!" I told her.

"Okay," she said tentatively. She knew the risk as well as I did, but she was also in a room with Brian and Rick at the time. There wasn't much she could say.

I didn't find out until later that Lesley already knew. Brian had ratted his parents out! When the meeting was over we stayed upstairs until we could see from the window that their car had pulled away. Then Lesley called Janet at DHS to let her know what had happened. Rick's next weekly visit was canceled as punishment.

"It really was an honest mistake, though," Janet said when I next spoke to her on the phone. "It's a long story, but one of their cars was in the shop and..."

"Janet," I said. "Remember what you know about Munchausen by Proxy mothers. They are very intelligent people. And they have a reason for everything. They can convince seasoned professionals."

"I know. I know. Anyway, Brian has a visit with his grandfather and his aunt and uncle next week Thursday. I can't be there so it will be supervised by my boss, Roger. He'll call you with a time and place."

"Okay..."

"You sound upset."

"Not upset. Just confused. How many people is he going to have visits with? He's already got his psychiatrist and his step dad once a week. I signed him up for the baseball team like you told me to. He'll have practices."

"This is just a one shot deal. They called begging, really. You can imagine how hard this is for them to accept. They've only known him as a sick kid. They just need to see for themselves."

"That makes sense. He's not on the team yet anyway. He has try-outs next week. I'm not sure he's going to make it, but I admire him for trying. We've been practicing in the park."

"We'll work visits around baseball if he makes the team."

It was Brian's second week in school. He reported that he was having a blast. From the second day I dropped him off, he had friends to join in hacky sack or just hanging around the steps. He ran out the front door after school and waved good-bye to a group of boys who had "geeks with potential to be heartthrobs after puberty" written all over them. Just the group I would expect to see Brian with. Sometimes he asked if a friend could come over and the two of them played video games or jumped on the trampoline until dinner.

It was heartwarming to see him doing so well. But it was also unnerving. It was as if he had always attended school, though I had been told he rarely did and even then it was in a wheelchair. Transitions that should have been jolting for Brian were seamless. Only on first meetings, like with his teachers or his psychiatrist, did I see a hint of shyness. He'd pull his baseball cap down over his eyes, answer in monosyllables for a few interactions, slouching. Then suddenly he'd smile his easy smile and snap out of it.

He loved to talk about sports, video games and paintball. He'd been working on me to buy him a paintball gun, and was finding the perfect purchase on the Internet as if he was doing me a favor by finding a good price. That was the usual depth of our conversations. He never brought up his unusual circumstances, and if anyone else did, his eyes opened wide with a hint of defensiveness, then he changed the subject.

It was Thursday, Brian's second week of school and his third week with me. I was picking him up from school, as usual, and taking him to his second meeting with his psychiatrist. Most kids got counselors. If they were on medications they saw a psychiatrist once in a while to renew meds. Brian got to see the far more educated and expensive psychiatrist once a week because his case was so bizarre and the possibilities for adjustment problems so great.

So far I had been faithful about driving him to school and picking him up. I circled the school a few times checking out license plates too. I usually left the house five minutes early for just that purpose, but that Thursday I was late. I just pulled up out front and waited. The bell would ring and kids would explode out of the big double doors at the top of the steps any minute. Brian would be easy to spot in his red fleece.

But he didn't show. I didn't get worried right away. He might have had a teacher to check with about homework or a friend to finish telling a story. It crossed my mind that I shouldn't have been late that day. What if his mother was outside the back door while I was waiting patiently out front? Nah. He'd be along.

The crowd thinned. I spotted one of his friends.

"Tim! Have you seen Brian?"

"Not since math."

I knew he didn't like me to get out of the car and look conspicuous but I did anyway. I stretched tall and tried to spot the red jacket from my new height. I looked at my watch. They could be ten minutes away by now. The Turnpike was ten minutes away.

I got in the car and drove around the back of the school. I circled one more time and parked. In the office I asked to have him paged over the loudspeaker. Each of his teachers was called over the intercom. None had met with him after class for any reason. He didn't answer the page.

My hands were shaking when I reached into my purse and pulled out a picture I'd taken of him on one of our hikes.

"Have you seen this boy?" I asked the office staff. "Did anyone come for him? Or did he get a phone call in school today? Anything?"

No one had any information.

I drove home. If he'd walked, he'd be there. If he was with her, they had a big head start. If he was with her, HE WOULD NOT SEE ADULTHOOD! DAMMIT! If he wasn't home, I'd call the state police, the DHS worker, the detective, and Lesley. Who else? Oh, yeah. Dr. Landry. His appointment was 5 minutes ago.

Stephen was home, but Brian wasn't. There were no messages on the answering machine. I called everyone on my list. It was tough to get the state police to understand how important this was.

"He's late coming home from school?" the dispatcher asked.

"He's a foster child. A kidnap risk. If his mother has him, she might kill him." I wanted to get to the describing the car and the clothes he was wearing. It was taking forever.

"You lost Brian?" Stephen kept asking.

I covered the phone with my hand. "Just a minute and I'll explain."

I finished all my phone calls and started the story, but he had heard it three times by then. "You lost him," he said conclusively.

It was an hour since I'd raced over to the school to get my usual parking spot and wait for Brian. Why didn't I go early and drive around? Why, that one day, was I late? Now I would never see Brian again. He would turn up in some Emergency Room in another state, seizing, vomiting, or comatose. Probably with a new name. I would never even know what happened to him. I would be one more person who let him slip through the cracks.

The phone kept ringing with yet another person wanting to hear how it happened. Lesley was trying to get out of a meeting to come over. I called my friend Carol for moral support.

Another hour went by. I couldn't believe this was happening.

The phone rang.

It was Brian. "Mary?" he said, timidly.

"Brian!" I shouted. "Where are you?"

"Kenny's."

"Who the hell is Kenny?"

"The kid with the paintball gun. He's letting me try it, but I don't think I want the same kind. The grip is a little…"

"Brian! Do you have any idea how many people are looking for you?"

"Why?"

"School was out hours ago! You had a doctor's appointment! I have been frantic!"

"Oh, yeah…sorry."

"Oh, my God!"

"Sorry," he said a little more convincingly.

"Look, I have a lot of people to call. Then I'll come and get you. Give me the number and I'll call back for directions. And listen, I won't hug you in front of your friends, but I'm hugging you as soon as we get home. You scared me to death."

"Am I grounded?"

"I'll get back to you on that."

I ran through my calling list a second time. In some instances I had to leave messages. As I was heading out the door to retrieve my lost charge, the phone rang and it was Janet.

"Apparently, he went out the back door of the school and walked over to a friend's house." I explained, breathless.

"I'm surprised you didn't just assume something like that had happened."

"What?" I said, not expecting that response.

"Isn't that pretty typical fourteen-year-old behavior?"

"This isn't a typical situation."

"Yes, but when you called me you said something like you'd had a bad feeling about today. I wonder if that's what made you overreact…"

I gasped. "Who am I speaking to?" I sputtered into the phone, truly confused for a minute.

She laughed nervously.

"Isn't this Janet?" I asked again.

"Yes."

"I had a bad feeling because I was late and didn't check out the neighborhood. I called the police because you told me to! YOU TOLD ME he was a kidnap risk!"

"Yes, but that was weeks ago."

"It changed?"

"Well, I think enough time has gone by. His parents have been doing everything they're told."

"Just a week ago she sat in a car and watched him walk into Agency B."

"And they explained that to me. It was an honest mistake and they've been punished for it. I don't think you have to worry about them."

"So he's not a kidnap risk?"

"Not any more."

"Thanks for telling me." She was silent for a moment.

"So he can walk to school from now on?" I asked.

"I think so."

And that incident set a precedent for the rest of the five months Brian lived with us. Flip-flop. Flip-flop.

CHAPTER 12

That Poor Child

It was just about a week later that I took Brian to the DHS offices to meet with his aunt, uncle and grandfather. Steve and I walked Brian in and shook hands with Roger, Janet's supervisor who would be in the room for the whole visit. He was a man about my age with curly red hair, charming enough that I took a quick look at his ring finger (old habits die hard). He asked if I had any questions and told me to feel free to call him if I ever did. I thought I just might and left Brian in his apparently competent hands.

An hour later, Stephen and I returned. This time we were introduced to Brian's relatives who also seemed like very nice people. As everyone said their good-byes, Roger repeated to the group of us that we should call him any time, and then he said to the relatives, "Janet will call you to set up next week's visit."

Startled by that last comment, I asked Brian about it as soon as we got in the car, "What's this about another visit? I thought this was it for a while."

"No, that guy said we were going to have weekly visits from now on."

"With all of them?"

"Yeah."

"And your dad too."

"Not together. My dad can only come on weekends."

"What about baseball? Did you mention that?"

"No. I don't know. I guess I'll have to skip a few practices."

The next day I put in a call to Janet to get to the bottom of the visit situation. She wasn't in, so I asked for Roger. I waited while the receptionist tried to track him down. After a bit she got back on the phone.

"He wants to know why you're calling," she said.

"To talk about Brian." Wasn't that obvious?

"What about Brian?"

"I'd like to talk to Roger about that directly if you don't mind."

Exasperated, she put me back on hold. Then after a minute, Roger's voice came on, booming.

"What's the problem?" he barked.

"I just wanted to clarify something you said yesterday. You said something about further visits. I was told yesterday's visit was a one shot deal and he may have baseball practice..."

He didn't let me finish. "Oh for heaven sakes!' he shouted. "These are the people he's going to be living with. Of course he's going to have weekly visits."

"They are?" I asked stunned. "I was told he was staying with me."

"He has a perfectly nice family who want to take him in. He will be moving as soon as possible and you will get him to the visits in the meantime. Is that clear?"

Baseball was no longer my concern. "Do you think he's safe there? They are his mother's family. Are they going to protect him from her?"

"They have signed a paper guaranteeing that they understand his mother is guilty and they will keep him from having any contact with her."

Later that afternoon I heard from the annoying secretary again. She said I wasn't to call Roger or even Janet again. They would call me.

Flip-flop. Call anytime. Don't ever call again. Brian is staying with us permanently. Brian is leaving very soon. Fortunately Janet graced me with a call the next day and I got to question her about the second one.

"Oh, it's way off in the future, if at all." she said when I asked how soon he would be leaving. "Family gets to name two possible kinship placements and then the department investigates them. In Brian's case it's Uncle Bill or Grandpa. Both are in another state. It's going to be months before the home study can even begin and we're going to make it take even longer. It's important when we go into court to be able to say Brian has been healthy for a significant period of time. We'd like to drag it all on so we can be talking about years, not months of good health."

"Okay," I said, reassured once again, "but I am curious. Who gets to pick what two family members are considered?"

"His mother."

"Doesn't that seem like the wrong person is calling the shots?"

"That's the way the law is written. But by the time Brian goes with them, she'll be in jail."

Two weeks later I got a phone call. The home study was finished and they passed with flying colors. Flip-flop-flip-flop.

One never knows for sure how long a foster child is staying. It is tough to deal with because there is a different way you relate to a child you expect to watch grow up than one whose stay is self-limited. While I know things can change for many reasons, I expect to be kept updated on the changes, if for no other reason, so I can temper my emotional involvement. And I expect the person giving me the news to respect that. Some do. Others apparently think heartbreak is part of what I get paid for.

Brian was tough to keep an emotional distance from. He was just too damn lovable. Even Stephen, who felt competitive with every other foster child he shared me with, worshipped Brian. He competed with me for time with Brian instead of the other way around!

Which is not to say Brian was easy. Pleasant, funny, talkative, intelligent…but not easy.

There is a term I knew from being a nurse and that is, "learned helplessness of the chronically ill." I'd dealt with the condition quite a bit during the years I worked as a pulmonary patient educator. To avoid shortness of breath, emphysema patients limit their activities, letting others do for them whenever possible. In the rehab classes I taught, they learned how to accomplish daily activities, minimizing shortness of breath with breathing techniques and exercise. They were always thrilled to get back what they had lost.

Brian was not thrilled to get back the ability to make a bed or do a homework assignment. When he met a few cute girls at school, he quit waiting for me to wash his face and did it himself, but that seemed to be all the responsibility he was willing to take. A typical evening in our house went like this:

"Brian, pick up your dishes and put them in the sink. In this household we all…"

"Okay, okay."

"Brian, where are you going?"

"To the bathroom."

"Put your dishes in the sink first."

"I'll be right back."

Later, "Brian, your dishes are still on the table."

"I'll be right there."

"Now."

"Next commercial. Hey! Turn the TV back on!"

"When your dishes are picked up."

"Fine. I've got homework to do anyway."

"After you pick up your dishes."

"So now you don't want me to do my homework? Okay, I'll just tell my teachers you wouldn't let me do it."

The teachers were hardly going to side with him against me. They were having the same experience I was having. That really surprised me. An evaluation done in the hospital, as well as my own observation, told me he was a very bright kid. I had also been told that when he was able to go to school, he was a star student. Eventually I realized that that information came by word-of-mouth only. Brian and his relatives reported that he was an "A" student. But records seemed to be impossible to locate. And those that did finally arrive indicated that he wasn't in school often enough to evaluate. Still, when he came home from school every day with glowing stories of the work he was accomplishing, I believed him.

Then the phone call came and a meeting with his teachers.

"He does absolutely nothing."

Mother or foster mother, I still felt responsible. My face turned red.

"He stares out the window when he is supposed to be doing work. When I tell him this is his only chance to finish it, he responds very politely, saying that he's going to do it, then goes right back to staring out the window. He doesn't seem the least bit embarrassed to have nothing to turn in."

Everyone I told of this problem had the same reaction. "That poor child! How can he possibly concentrate after all he's been through?" Only his teachers and I saw it differently. Probably because we saw his demeanor during the episodes of non-compliance. We didn't see the face of depression, confusion or distraction. We saw a power struggle.

Even without that, I felt it was time to stop seeing him as "that poor child." Sure, he'd been through a lot, as every foster child has. But the pattern of his life so far was one of getting away with anything he wanted to get away with because he was "that poor child." Who would give an "F" to a child with a terminal illness? Who would expect a dying child to pick up after himself? Now he expected the same consideration because he was "that poor child" whose mother tried to kill him. I felt, and his teachers felt, that at 14 there was very little time to waste letting him continue to be "that poor child."

Brian slept well. He ate well. He was growing like a weed. And he had plenty of energy to jump on the trampoline or play hacky sack. He taught Stephen a hilarious hula girl routine that they loved to do for visiting social workers. He showed no signs of being devastated by the things that had happened in his life. Except for his profound laziness.

We had the typical parent/child discussions on the subject. He nodded in agreement about his need to take more responsibility. He wrinkled up his nose at the part about potential consequences of his behavior. But nothing changed.

Lesley suggested I call Brian's psychiatrist, which I did. I had met Dr. Landry at the hospital on the day I brought Brian home. I knew others were happy to have her involved as she had a very good reputation for her work with children. I found her pleasant on our first meeting and had every reason to believe she would be helpful to all of us. I was shocked to learn she did not consider that to be in her job description.

I left a message for her to call me while Brian was at school on a Monday. I waited, checked my messages every time I came back from an errand, and waited some more. When she hadn't called by his Thursday appointment, I made a point of walking in with him instead of dropping him off at the door. She looked disturbed to see me, but asked if I needed to speak with her alone. I said yes and followed her as she scurried down the long hall to her office.

"I'm very uncomfortable with this," she said, as soon as the door was closed.

"You are?"

"I intentionally didn't return your phone call. It's very important that Brian and I develop a relationship separate from his relationships with everyone else. We need to develop a trust between us. He is never going to trust me if he thinks I talk about him behind his back."

"Does he tell you how well things are going, that he is doing great work in school?"

"Yes."

"Then he is lying to you, too. He's not doing well at all."

"He needs to be in here for this discussion. I shouldn't know anything about him that he hasn't told me himself. If you have a concern, you need to tell it to me in front of him."

Brian knew why I had come in with him. I actually expected us to go in together to talk about it, but when she asked if I needed to talk alone, I assumed that meant she did. I thought it was her idea. I quickly realized the only reason she wanted to talk alone was to lay down the ground rules. When Brian joined us, I repeated my concerns about school. I told her for the first time that he was failing every subject.

"Not any more," he piped up. "I turned in my late work to everyone except Mr. Berger. I can't catch up in his class because he won't tell me what I need to do."

"Brian, that's not true. He gave me a list of things you need to do to catch up and I gave it to you."

"But that list was wrong. I had already done that work. I've tried to talk with him after class and he won't talk to me. It's his mistake. Talk to anyone. Everyone hates him."

I knew Brian was blatantly lying. Mr. Berger was the most organized teacher I'd ever met. His assignments were written on the board with due dates. Each had a corresponding box of study material that kids were free to take home. Names were crossed off as each assignment was turned in. And he had regular office hours every day. Plus I had double-checked with his homeroom teacher late that day. He was still failing everything.

"Maybe you can intercede for Brian with Mr. Berger," Dr. Landry said before I could go on.

"Brian has turned in no assignments. Not to Mr. Berger or anyone else. I talked to the teachers today."

"They just haven't gone through all their papers yet," he said. "I worked on stuff in study hall today. It's all turned in except for Berger's. And he's impossible."

I looked at Dr. Landry hoping it was obvious to her what was going on. It wasn't.

"Is there another teacher in that subject area?" she asked me. "Can he transfer to someone with more understanding?"

I couldn't tell if this was sincere, in which case we were back to "the poor child," or if siding with him was just an essential strategy in gaining his trust. But I could see that I'd come to the wrong place. Score one for Brian. He finished the school year with mostly D's and F's.

Surprisingly, Brian and I were able to maintain a pretty decent relationship in spite of these issues. He didn't hold it against me that I complained to his doctor about him and I didn't hold it against him that he made me look like a fool.

CHAPTER 13

Good Days and Bad

One evening Brian ran downstairs calling my name, waving me over to the living room window. There was an ambulance at a house down the street with its lights flashing and a lot of activity surrounding it.

"Don't you just love ambulances?!" he said, enraptured.

"No," I answered honestly. "Not really."

"I do," he said, the red light waving over his face like a heartbeat.

"What do you love about ambulances?" I asked. "I'd think you'd have had some pretty bad experiences in them by now."

"Oh, no, I've had good experiences."

"Like what?"

"Once I got a pen cap stuck in my lungs and they had to take me to the hospital. It was so cool...the siren...everyone getting out of your way."

"A pen cap! How old were you?"

"Eleven."

"How does an eleven-year-old inhale a pen cap?"

I couldn't see how this connected with his supposed illness or his mother's real one.

"I had it between my teeth and I laughed. It went right down into my lungs and blocked one of them off completely. They had to stick this tube down to get it out."

"In the ambulance?"

"No. Once I got to the hospital."

"Weren't you choking in the ambulance? How could that have been a good experience?"

"I don't know. It was just cool. And later my mother wrote a letter to the company that made the pen. That cap was the exact size of a child's windpipe. We could have sued them, but my mom just wanted them to stop making that cap. They wrote a letter thanking her and changed the whole design of the pen."

I couldn't keep my mouth shut. "Brian, how many sizes of children are there?"

"What do you mean?"

"How many sizes are there of children? That's how many sizes there are of children's windpipes. They'd have to take all pen caps off the market."

"Well, I don't know," he answered, a bit disgruntled. "All I know is I saw the letter."

Official-looking letterhead is almost as easy to come by as Syrup of Ipecac, I thought to myself. But I had already said enough. It was my goal to make him think, not to do the thinking for him. Lord knows he had me thinking. How did she get a foreign object down his lungs in the first place? Or, did he do it? It wasn't the first time it crossed my mind that Brian might have been complicit in at least some of her game.

Before I met Brian, when I had only heard his story, I thought he had to have some awareness of what was going on. He was too old not to. I wondered if he would wait until he felt safe and tell everything he knew. Or if he was too enmeshed with his mother to see it as wrong and would keep covering for her. If she was doing it for the attention, from doctors and other strangers, maybe he was going along with it for attention from her. Obviously, he couldn't be blamed for going along with it, no matter what his frame of mind. It was the only life he ever knew.

When I first laid eyes on him, with his big, brown eyes and pale, knobby fingers, all thoughts of his involvement left my head. He just looked so innocent, so "victim-like." But that was short-lived.

Now I was back to being quite certain he knew more than he was telling. The story about the pen cap was just one of many that convinced me. Once we came across a rock climbing wall and he began to regale us with tales of his own experiences climbing mountains.

"When did you climb mountains?" I asked, thinking it was years earlier, before the really sick years.

"Last summer."

"Weren't you in a wheelchair last summer?"

He looked at me over his shoulder and winked. "I had good days and bad."

It was the wink that threw me. I could see where his mother might have drugged him more some days than others. And an unsophisticated observer might have thought it was just a matter of good days and bad days. Brian could have been convinced that it was the normal course of his disease that on good days he could climb mountains but on bad days he couldn't even lift his head. But wouldn't she have had to tell him not to tell his doctors about the really good days, the mountain-climbing days? They would certainly have been suspicious. Especially since they signed papers sending him to Disney World in a wheelchair, courtesy of the Make-a-Wish Foundation that same summer. He must have been instructed to stay in that wheelchair whenever the Make-a-Wish people were around. That cloak of secrecy about his "good days" must have been why he winked.

The other thing that was becoming clear to me was that attention wasn't the only motivation for his mother. There was also material gain involved both for her and for Brian. She was from a wealthy family. Brian's father was an older man with a blue-collar job and a drinking problem. She divorced him and married Rick, a UPS driver. They lived in a beautiful house on the ocean. Her father was paying for it. He wanted Brian to be able to see the water from his sickbed.

It didn't take long to see how much material goods meant to Brian. He talked about it constantly. He didn't just have a baseball glove. He had a $245 baseball glove. He didn't want to ride one of our bikes. He had a $600 bike at home, his home on the ocean. When we got a cocker spaniel puppy to ease his sadness over missing his dog, he wanted to go to L.L. Bean for a $200 dog bed. Everything had a price tag on it. Even food. Once he asked if we could have Ducktrap salmon for supper. "It's the most expensive brand," he told me, "the only kind I eat."

And he had conned me into buying him a paintball gun, telling me an uncle had agreed to pay me back through his step dad on his next visit. The uncle had even agreed to the expensive one or so Brian said. I did as I was told, then the check never came. Every Saturday there was a new excuse why Rick didn't bring my money. Of course, I never talked to Rick myself. The visits were supervised by a social worker, and I just dropped Brian off and picked him up. It was early in my understanding of Brian and I didn't think to question his honesty, but I learned from the person supervising the visits that there was no such conversation about anyone paying me back for the paintball gun. When I learned this, I took the gun back, much to Brian's consternation.

"Can't you just say, 'This one's on me?'" he asked.

"What do you mean?"

"It's a gift. It's my birthday present. You know you missed my birthday."

"I didn't even know you on your birthday."

"That's my point! You know me now and you owe me a birthday present."

"Then you owe me a birthday present too. How many years back are we going to go with this, because you'll owe me more presents than I'll owe you."

"I can't believe you won't just give me the gun!"

"Brian, you lied to me. You're not going to be rewarded for it." I had to add a little lesson in the obvious. "I'm sure you're not used to being told no. No one is going to say no to a dying kid. But you're not dying anymore. You're healthy and growing and doing things you've never done before. You've got a future. That's the good part. The bad part is you're not going to get away with stuff you've been getting away with." I took the gun and he never saw it again.

Then one day the boys and I were sitting on the trampoline telling stories. I often climbed up there after the boys were tired from jumping and sat in the sun with them and our new dog, Ginkgo. Steve and Brian were both curious about me and used to ask me to tell them stories from my life. I would ask what kind of story and they would pick something like, my childhood, or a hospital story or a raising Tony and Renee story. That particular day, they asked for an ex-husband story. I was only too happy to provide one.

On a subconscious level, I might have chosen the particular story because of what it would mean to Brian, but consciously I was halfway through it before I saw the connection. I considered changing the ending, but I was in too deep by then. It was a long story, about my ex-brother-in-law and his crazy wife Rita. But the short version is that Rita pretended to have rheumatoid arthritis for years, so that Aunt Anna (referred to as Aunt Megabucks behind her back) would keep sending them money. She sent them $35,000 as a down payment on a house. She bought them a car and sent them on cruises.

It was years before Richard and I realized Rita wasn't really sick.

"What did you do?" Stephen asked me.

"Nothing." I answered. "There was nothing to do. But I was a little jealous. I would have loved a new car, or a big chunk of money to put down on a house. Rich and I started talking about it, trying to figure out if we could play the game better, get some of Aunt Anna's money."

"Did you?"

"No. In the end, I just couldn't be that dishonest. It's tempting, but I couldn't do it."

"Oh yes, you could," Brian said, with a sly little smile on his face. "It's easy."

"Well, it wouldn't be worth it, having to keep up the pretense all the time."

"It's worth it," Brian answered. "Believe me, it's worth it."

He could NOT have been more clear. In that brief exchange, he told me all I needed to know about his involvement. He played along for the material rewards. He must have thought that his mother would never really let him die, that it was a game, but a safe one. Didn't he ever stop and think that a person can only have a dying child for so long? Eventually it would have to end. It was ending when the ICU doctor finally saw the light and intervened.

Someone had to talk to him. Someone had to set him straight. I wasn't supposed to.

Lesley, my Agency B social worker, was the first person I called whenever Brian revealed himself to me. She, like me, was charmed by his personality, fascinated by his circumstances and terrified for his future. She, like me, had read up on Munchausen by Proxy Syndrome and knew that if his mother got him back again, either because the court case went her way, or by some devious method, she would have to kill him. She would have to leave the state with him, cause a "relapse" somewhere where she wasn't known to be a phony, and take his life.

Even if he didn't end up back with his mother, his prognosis was grim. Lesley and I both read the statement on the Internet that there were no reported cases of MBP survivors growing up to be normal healthy adults. They were all severely damaged as adults. Maybe we should have given up on Brian then and there. But we couldn't. We wanted him to be the first to make it.

It was good to have Lesley to bounce things off of. But in the end, she didn't have any more decision-making power than I did. In theory, she did have the ear of the decision makers. She was at least allowed to call DHS directly. But they rarely returned her calls.

There was one piece of information I was nearly desperate to get to DHS. It was about Brian's first unsupervised visit with his relatives. It had come quickly. I'd been told it would be months before visits were unsupervised. In a typical DHS flip-flop, the Mother's Day visit became the first, just ten weeks after Brian moved in with me.

"Why so soon?" I asked when Janet made one of her rare phone calls to me to tell me this weekend's visit would be four hours long instead of the usual one, and that they would be taking Brian out instead of staying in the DHS visitation room.

"Well, the Uncle called and he said it wasn't very natural, sitting in that little room."

"So that was it? He asked, therefore he got?"

"What do you think is going to happen?" she asked rhetorically. "He's the vice-president of a bank."

Nothing drastic did happen. They went to the mall and Brian seemed fine when Steve and I picked him up afterwards. He even bought me a Mother's Day present, a stuffed bear holding a plastic rose.

But, when Steve went to bed that night, at the very first moment Brian could talk to me without Steve around, he said, "Guess what we did at the mall today? We bought my mom a Mother's Day present."

"Oh," I answered, at a loss for the right response. "Was that your idea?" I finally managed to ask.

"No, my Grandpa's. He said they would be seeing her on Tuesday so they would give it to her then."

"How'd you feel about that?"

"I don't know."

There was an uncomfortable silence as we headed downstairs to watch TV.

"Why?" he finally asked.

"Why what?"

"Why did you ask how I feel about it?"

"Well, I noticed you told me as soon as Steve wasn't around, like you wanted to talk about it or something."

"No. I only just thought about it then. That's all."

I was stunned that Brian's family would so brazenly break the rule of no contact between Brian and his mother. Sending a gift seemed like contact to me, and it was certainly an indication that they didn't intend to keep the two of them apart.

Lesley agreed and began placing phone calls to Janet to fill her in before the next weekend's visit. They were able to connect quickly for once and Janet reacted just as we did. She said the unsupervised visits would stop, maybe the supervised ones as well. I breathed a sigh of relief when Lesley got back to me on it. But my warm fuzzy was short-lived.

"We'll be talking more about it at the team meeting next week," Lesley told me.

"There's a team meeting?!" I asked, flustered. "I don't think I have it on my calendar. Did I get a notice?"

"No," she said. "You're not invited. But don't feel too bad. I wasn't either at first. I had to get the director here to call and insist that I be included."

"Oh, my God!" I shouted, stunned by the audacity. "How can they discuss Brian without us there? They have no idea how he's doing!"

"I know. I know. They think Dr. Landry can best speak to how Brian is doing."

"He doesn't tell her anything! He lied about how he's doing at school!"

"I know. His GAL will be there, too. She's met with him, hasn't she?"

"Once…weeks ago." I answered. I was pleased originally when Vickie got assigned as Brian's GAL because she was a lawyer and obviously intelligent, but for some inexplicable reason she had fallen hook, line and sinker for Brian's mother. She visited her, talked to her on the phone, even called me once to tell me that Brian's mother said I shouldn't let Brian ride a bike alone because he got splitting headaches and could have an accident. Being a delayed reactor, my immediate response was to agree to watch him more carefully. Then I remembered, HIS MOTHER TRIED TO KILL HIM! I wasn't going to give a message to Brian from her that essentially said, "Start having your headaches again, honey."

I was wild, after hearing the team meeting would be held without me. I wasn't sure what the message was. The least insulting possibility was that I was irrelevant to the process. It was also possible that the meeting was about me, and how I was a hindrance to the process. Agency B was sending two representatives, Lesley and the director of the agency. Did I need that much defending?

I got a call from Janet the week before the meeting, just days after Lesley reported to her that Brian had purchased a Mother's Day present for his mother. She called to say that the next weekend's visit would go as planned, four hours, unsupervised.

"I talked to his uncle and he said they bought the Mother's Day present for you, not for his real mother."

"They got one for me, too. But Brian said they got something for his mother and that Grandpa agreed to give it to her on Tuesday."

"What was it?"

"He didn't say."

"I think Brian's toying with you."

"He told his pediatrician too, Dr. Gordon. He had an appointment with her this morning and he brought it up."

"Did he tell her what the gift was?"

"No."

"I think he made it up."

"Why would he do that?" I asked, "I mean, even if he did, he would have to know that it reflects badly on his family and he might not have any more unsupervised visits. That would seem to be his goal, whether he is telling the truth or making it up."

Janet paused. "I know it's tempting to try to interpret his behavior. But why don't you leave that to the professionals."

When I relayed the story to Lesley later, I added sarcastically, "Why don't I just leave the thinking to the big brains!"

"Calm down," she told me.

CHAPTER 14

✦ ✦ ✦

Foster Caretaking

My heart was pounding for the entire two hours the meeting was supposed to be going on. It was pounding even harder for the next hour while I waited for a phone call from Lesley with a report.

How had I become the enemy here? By calling too much? By asking too many questions? Brian was a treatment level child and not a typical one. I couldn't do it by myself. I needed that "village" Hillary Clinton wrote about. In theory, that's what our team was. But I was doing all the work, taking all the risks, and they got to do all the "thinking." It was my heart that was going to be broken if things went badly with Brian. Not theirs.

Lesley didn't call that day. Was the meeting going on that long, or was she delaying giving me upsetting news? I called first thing the next morning and got her voice mail. Finally around noon, her boss Karen called. That meant diplomacy was called for. Karen was a master of diplomacy. But she wasn't even at the meeting. The information she was giving me was second hand.

"Mary, I know you've been waiting for this call," she said. "I'm sorry it's taken so long. It wasn't an easy meeting."

"I didn't think it would be."

"You've never seen so many strong personalities in one room, but Marguerite is no shrinking violet either, you know. She held her own." She was referring to the agency head.

"Well?"

113

"I'm told each person there had very strong opinions on what should happen with Brian. No one was listening to anyone else. The GAL is quite sure he'd be safe back with his mother and wants to recommend that visits with her begin immediately."

"Good Lord!"

"DHS wasn't going to let that happen. Janet even said she was going to let the home study sit on her desk without a signature as long as possible to keep him in foster care. That's one good thing."

"I hear a 'but...'"

"They don't think he ever told you he bought a present for his mother."

"They think I'm lying!?"

"He denied it, according to Dr. Landry."

"Did they call his pediatrician to confirm it? I told Janet that he told Dr. Gordon too."

"Apparently not."

"So unsupervised visits will continue. I expected that. What else went on?"

"Well, Dr. Landry is pretty much refusing to testify in the case because she says it would undermine Brian's trust if he knew she was testifying."

"Janet must has been livid! She's been counting on that testimony."

"She essentially threatened to force her. She said she could subpoena her, or even change therapists if she had to, though it's pretty late in the game for that."

"Oh, my Lord! So at least I'm not the only bad guy."

"Oh, no. There wasn't a single bit of agreement in that room. It's as if everyone owns Brian and no one is willing to share. Everyone has their own take, and that is the only one that counts."

"That could describe me as well. I feel like I'm the only one who understands what's going on and what should be going on."

"No, but you're trying very hard to share the information you have. Everyone else is playing it close to the vest, giving only the information they have to give and expecting everyone to go along with their recommendations anyway. But in the end, DHS doesn't have to listen to any of them. The GAL isn't going to get what she wants. Dr. Landry is going to be forced to testify."

"Did it sound like any of them has bothered to educate themselves on the syndrome? I mean, are they quoting from the literature on the subject or just flying by the seat of their pants?"

"I don't think anyone has read as much as you and Lesley have."

"Well, I've been on the Internet and I managed to leave an email for the author of one of the books I've read on the subject. He called me just last night and when I told him about Brian and the plan to put him with his mother's family. He said it was a big mistake."

"Really?"

"He referred me to a nurse/counselor named Louise Lasher who specializes in MBP and I looked at her website. She is very clear on that point."

"Wow. You know, I wish I could say I think someone would care if you gave them that information."

"I guess they've been pretty clear on that. So what else did they say about me?" It was time to bite the bullet.

"Not that much, like I said, they're all more concerned about themselves than anyone else. But I do think you need to see this case a little differently than most."

Here it was, the part she was waiting to tell me, as diplomatically as possible. "How's that?"

"You need to see yourself more as a caretaker than a parent. Your job really is just to feed him and get him to the places he needs to go."

"So who is doing the parenting then?"

"Janet said he is to call DHS if he needs to talk or has any problems. Or he can talk to Dr. Landry. You are to direct him to call one of them."

Interesting. That was how my mother did foster care and I always said I wanted to do it differently. She always had plenty of food in the house, a TV in every bedroom. She expected to do a lot of driving. But she never really got to know each child. Come to think of it, that was pretty much how she raised her own kids. She used to joke that by the time she realized one of us was having problems, we had usually solved them ourselves. She had eight kids of her own.

I, on the other hand, had two. And the first one was diagnosed as autistic and retarded by the time he was a toddler. I immersed myself in that subject until I was able to prove that diagnosis wrong. That was the way I liked to parent. That was my idea of good parenting. But then, I wasn't supposed to parent here, just caretaker.

I was at my boiling point. "You know, I have just about had it with this case."

"I don't blame you."

"Brian may be charming, but he is not easy. He still expects to be waited on hand and foot. And I can't get anywhere with that because while I'm trying to have words with him about picking up after himself, the doorbell rings and it's the mailman with more presents for him. His family sees him every weekend. They send him home with armloads of presents and then they still mail him more in between. How do you think that feels to Stephen? He's the good kid in this household. He has made so much progress this spring and he hasn't got 2000 Pokemon cards, and counting. They've made it practically impossible to parent Brian anyway. The only thing I do besides feed him and take him where he needs to be is listen when he wants to talk about his situation. And now I'm not supposed to do that either. What is the point here? Why am I taking this crap?"

"I don't know. I'm not sure I would."

It is so hard to turn around and say, "Hi! How was school?" to a child walking in the door when you've just been kicked in the gut again by his "team." When I looked at Brian, my heart went out to him and I just wanted to keep him safe. When I talked to his "team" or got secondhand messages from them I wanted to drop him off on their doorstep and say, "He's all yours."

But before I had much time to consider my options, we had a whole new issue. Shortly after the infamous team meeting, I got a call from Lesley. Janet had called her to say that Brian's great-grandmother was dying and she wanted to talk to Brian before she died. Janet had given permission. Lesley gave me a name and phone number. I was to listen on the other phone while he talked to assure that it wasn't just a ruse to get him to talk to his mother.

"It's kind of bizarre, when you think about it," Lesley added. "You're supposed to monitor his phone call and yet he's off with her family for four hours every weekend. He could be talking to her the whole four hours."

When Brian got home, I gave him the information. He shook his head. "She's not sick," he said without hesitation.

"How do you know?"

"I just asked my dad last weekend how she was. He said she was fine."

"Old people get sick very quickly, Brian. They said she has lung cancer. I can tell you from experience, diagnosis to death can be very swift with that disease."

"She's not really sick," he repeated.

"Are you saying you think they're lying?"

"Yes."

"Why would they do that?"

"I don't know." It was clear he was not interested in continuing the discussion. By then he had his back to me as he was rummaging through the cupboards for an after school snack.

"Okay, Brian. I'll drop the subject, but I just want you to think about one thing."

He grunted.

"If it is true, and she dies, how are you going to feel?"

He grunted again, tearing open a bag of potato chips.

"I have the number if you decide to call. But I won't push it, okay?"

"Okay."

I was astounded. Of course, I called Lesley to report it the very next day. She immediately changed her plans for the afternoon and came out to the house.

I have to admit at first, I took it as an insult. As if I hadn't tried hard enough to talk him into making the call. I realized later, she was there to verify my findings, not question them. And wouldn't you know, I would end up needing a witness.

Brian had his usual appointment with Dr. Landry that Thursday. I thought she needed to help him get to the bottom of why he didn't call. I knew she wouldn't return my call if I tried to reach her by phone so I decided to accompany him to her office as I had done that one other time. The evening before, I discussed it with Brian.

"I feel like we need to talk with Dr. Landry about your great-grandmother, Brian. I thought I'd go in with you tomorrow, if that's all right."

"What's to talk about?"

"I guess it just seems a little strange to me that you don't trust the people who called to say she is sick. I think you need to explore that, but maybe with someone other than me. That's what a psychiatrist is for."

"Is that what she's for?" he said sarcastically.

"Sure. With all that's happened to you, we assume you have a lot to get to the bottom of. She is a safe person you can do that with."

"I don't tell her that kind of thing."

"Would you start, please? For me. I'm having a little trouble being the bearer of all emotional stuff from you, Brian. They don't always believe me."

"Like when?"

"Like when you said you got your mother a Mother's Day present. Your Uncle Bill denies it."

"Why does anybody care about that?"

"I care about it. It makes me concerned that they won't protect you from your mother like they have promised they would."

"They won't let me see her. I can promise you that. Because they don't want to break any rules and lose me."

"But do they understand that you need protecting from her?"

"You mean do they believe she did it?"

"Yeah."

"No, they definitely don't believe she did it. But they are going to say anything they have to say to get me out of foster care."

My heart sank, yet again.

The next day, we walked into Dr. Andrew's office and I explained why I was there. I wrapped up my story and she turned to Brian and asked why he didn't want to call.

He blinked as if he was taken by surprise by the conversation. "I just didn't know which Great grandmother it was. If it's Ruth, of course, I'll call."

"Brian!" I said, shocked. "You knew exactly who..."

"Well, I guess it was just a failure to communicate," the doctor interrupted.

He got me again. "So are you going to call her, Brian?" I asked.

"Sure," he said with wide-eyed innocence.

I asked about calling again when we got home. He shook his head no and went up to his room.

The next day, the news came. Great-grandma Ruth had died.

When I gave Brian that information, he looked upset. But his friend Kenny showed up at the door seconds later so we didn't get a chance to talk. Kenny asked why he looked mad and he said, "How would you feel? I just found out my great-grandmother died and I didn't even get a chance to say good-bye."

Later, after Kenny left, he was still in a bad mood.

"My parents are going to be so mad at me for not calling," he said.

The damn situation was so complex I hardly knew where to go with it so I finally said, "Brian, I know you're upset about your grandmother and I don't blame you. But let's put it in perspective. She was an old woman. It was her time to die. YOU almost died a few months ago," I said, pointing to his chest. "I find that way more upsetting. And as far as you not calling. I don't think anyone has a right to question your decision after all you've been through. Anyway, wherever Grandma Ruth is now, she understands why you didn't call."

"I didn't almost die," he muttered under his breath.

I took a deep breath. "Do you know what DNR means?"

"No."

"It means Do Not Resuscitate. It means let this person die, there is no hope anymore. You were a DNR."

He looked shocked in a way I had never seen before, as if maybe, it was the first time he really was. "I was?!"

"Brian, your funeral arrangements were made last November."

"No shit!"

"No shit."

What was I supposed to do, refer him to his DHS worker for that conversation? To be honest, I was glad to get a chance to give him that information. If he was going back into the bosom of his family, he needed to know the truth and be prepared to protect himself.

The next day, I picked him up from his supervised visit with his step dad, Rick. I'd worried about him the whole time, knowing he would have to explain why he didn't call Ruth.

"Did you talk about Grandma Ruth?" I asked.

"Yeah, I just told him no one told me she was sick."

"Brian!"

"What?" he asked casually.

"He's going to know soon enough that's not true. You talked to Dr. Landry and Lesley about it."

"So? I'll just keep denying it. What are they going to do? Call me a liar?"

"That works for you?"

"So far," he chuckled.

Thank goodness for Lesley. When the furious phone calls began on Monday, I was exonerated.

CHAPTER 15

Negotiations

After the kids went to bed at night, I was back to the computer and Freecell again. This case was just getting to be too much for me. My head was spinning. I needed to zone out. But I found myself staring at the computer screen and thinking about Brian instead, trying to figure out how things got to the place they were.

Where at first I was flattered at being chosen for this child, I now felt insulted at every turn.

"Don't call us, we'll call you."

"You overreacted."

"Leave the thinking to us."

And the worst was being considered a liar. Or maybe that wasn't the worst. The worst was that Brian was going back into the bosom of a family that could be very dangerous to him and I wasn't able to stop it.

I felt strongly that he was also afraid. While I knew by now that he was manipulative and dishonest, I also felt there was a common theme in the things he told me and no one else, the things he often later denied. That theme was that he was also afraid. The people who did listen, Lesley and Karen, agreed. But the people who needed to listen had blocked all communication. I wasn't invited to meetings and was told not to call DHS and Dr. Landry. Lesley left voice mail messages for Janet at DHS when I reported something Brian had said that I thought was important. But feedback told me they gave no credence to it.

I could give up. Or I could try one more thing, good old-fashioned letter writing. I switched the computer to word processing mode.

I tried to make what I was seeing clear in a letter. I retold the stories of the Mother's Day present, refusing to call Grandma Ruth, and his statement that his family would say what they had to say to get him back but they didn't believe it.

I also pointed out that each team member saw Brian no more than once a week. Most saw him less than once a month. They spent an hour and each asked the same two questions: Did he believe his mother was guilty and did he want to go back with family. His reported answers were no and yes. His reported affect was flat. I asked them to consider what they were asking of him, to deny his own family, the only family he had ever known.

I even quoted Ann Landers, who had said in her column once, "Don't spit on a well you may drink from yet." They were asking him to rat on his own family, knowing one member had tried to kill him and with no guarantee he would then be protected from it happening again.

I said that I felt he was telling his emotional truth to me, the only person he really talked to, the only person who saw him when he was really himself, animated and happy. And that emotional truth was that he wasn't ready to go back to family.

I reported that he talked to others as if he was staying with us forever. He asks what high school he will be going to, what we will be doing for Christmas. When the subject of moving in with his aunt and uncle came up, his gaze would drop to the ground and his voice would trail off.

I asked them to slow down on the visitation schedule and rethink the direction we were going with him. I sent a copy to each team member.

The next communication was a call from Karen, the diplomacy specialist. Brian's next family visit would be eight hours, not four. I was wild.

I sputtered and spit and threatened to quit again, and she did her usual thing, acknowledging my frustration and then pumping up my ego a little bit to help me go on. I went back to Freecell.

Then she surprised me by calling back a few hours later. "I spoke to Marguerite after I talked to you," she said. "And she had another take on things. She thinks maybe it's time to stop threatening to quit and prove you mean it."

"You mean give notice?"

"Yes. I didn't agree at first, but once I listened to her point of view, I think she may be right. Marguerite made it very clear in that meeting that they were threatening Brian's placement by treating you the way they do. And it hasn't changed anything. Maybe it is time to give up, or at least to force them to listen."

"You mean give notice but be willing to take it back if they make some changes. Like an ultimatum?"

"I wouldn't put it in the form of an ultimatum. No one ever responds positively to that. But if you just say you're quitting and state why, it will force them to think of ways to keep you. They don't want to move him now. Or, maybe they do want to move him. Maybe this is just a complete mismatch and this gives them an opportunity to fix it. Leave it in their hands."

I sat down to the computer and wrote the next letter. It was shorter and more to the point. I said I couldn't participate any more in something so destructive, not only to Brian, but to the rest of my family and to myself. I gave my two weeks notice. It was one of the most painful things I have ever done.

I sent a copy of my letter to the group at Agency B for their approval, and then it went out. A week later I was on a 3-way conference call negotiating a deal.

Lesley was on one phone and Roger, the supervisor, was on the other. I had four requirements in order to rescind my letter. I had to have them written down on a scrap of paper in front of me to keep Roger from making me so nervous I'd forget.

1. The department would consult a national specialist on MBP.
2. We would be assigned a counselor who *would* speak with me and who would work on family issues and behavior issues.
3. The presents from family would stop.
4. The unsupervised visits would stop.

Roger was pleasant through most of the conversation, but I could tell it was forced. He made a point of thanking me for finding the national specialist and asked me to send all the information I had to Janet. He agreed wholeheartedly that the presents had to stop, that it was impossible to run a household with two children being treated so differently. And he agreed to pay for the second counselor. I had a name of someone I wanted to see, a name I had been given my Stephen's

DHS worker. When it came the fourth issue, the unsupervised visits, he just said, "That's not going to happen. The visits are just going to get longer until he moves in with them at the end of the summer. We have no choice in that matter."

I could have said, fine, then find him a new foster home, but I didn't. I thought if he talked to the national specialist, she would be able to have some effect on that decision. We almost ended the conversation on a good note, when I said, "When do you think these things will be accomplished?"

"What?"

"If I am going to agree to keep Brian on the basis of these things you've agreed to do, I need to know when they will be done."

Roger yelled so loud, I didn't even understand him. I was holding the phone away from my ear by the end of his outburst. It was something to the effect that he was not going to be accused of a lack of integrity and if that was all the faith I had in his word then they would just find Brian a new placement.

Lesley jumped in. "I think what Mary is saying is that she has been promised things before and they have not happened. We need to be able to say the letter is rescinded unless these things are done by a certain date."

Roger was still upset. "Do you think you own any of this?" he bellowed.

I was babbling incoherently by then, and he continued shouting. Lesley jumped in again and said we have an agreement; we just need a date from him.

"This is not the only case I have," he shouted, though a little tamer. "It won't be today. It might not be tomorrow. I will get to it some time next week."

Lesley said, "Then is next Friday a good day to say it will all be done by?"

"Yes, it will all be done by next Friday."

"And if it isn't, the letter goes into effect on that day. Does that seem fair?" Lesley continued.

"All right," he groused.

"So I guess that's it. Thank you." but Roger had hung up by then. Lesley explained to me later that when he asked if I "owned" any of this, he meant any of the problems. I mistook him to be asking if I owned

Brian and my answer was idiotic. I would have loved to hear how he thought I owned some of the problems we were having. Well, maybe.

Later, I was so exhausted by the whole thing that I started to cry while I was talking to Brian about something else entirely. I tried to explain a little, but he turned back to the TV. I went up to my room for a while.

By the next Friday, I was seeing the counselor I wanted to see, and feeling much less alone. They did not contact Louise Lasher, the national specialist on MBP, but I had no way of knowing that. Unfortunately, I had forgotten in the negotiations that no one on the team spoke to me so there would be little way of finding out. I did run into one of the pediatricians who cared for Brian when he was in the hospital later that summer and he was quite cool to me. I wasn't sure why until he said, "I hear you asked that a national specialist on MBP be consulted."

"I did."

"Did you know I am a specialist in MBP?"

"No."

"Well, I am."

"Did they consult you?"

"I'm already on the case. I don't need to be consulted," he said and spun away. I didn't have a chance to ask what his involvement was since I hadn't even been aware of it.

The presents from family continued. I finally resorted to hiding them.

CHAPTER 16

Finding Jesse's Grave

The summer was a better time for us as a family. Steve went to day camp and Brian was more willing to help with yard work than he was with housework. In the evening we took our cocker spaniel, Ginkgo Biloba (I swear, the boys named him), to the dog park and let him run with other dogs. The boys climbed trees and I chatted with other dog owners.

The dog park was actually an old cemetery and quite the local controversy. Some people thought it was disrespectful to let dogs run all over the graves, leaving their droppings behind. Personally, I thought the dead would like to know so much life went on above them, but I can't speak for the dead.

One day Brian asked if I thought his brother Jesse's grave was there. "I doubt it."

"It might be. I know he's buried close to the Medical Center and that's right up the street."

"Why would he be buried here? Your parents didn't live here."

"They did then."

"Really!? I didn't know that. Then why was your brother in a hospital three hours away when he died?"

"My mom thought all the doctors here were jerks."

Brian might well have questioned how I knew what hospital his brother died in. He didn't know that I had discovered that Jesse was the subject of a medical journal article on Munchausen by Proxy Syndrome. The police detective told me about it on her first visit and I waited for Brian to start school to sneak off to the medical library and read it.

Jesse's case was one of the first recognized, though recognized too late to save his life. It was twelve years earlier when most doctors didn't realize medical child abuse existed.

The three-year-old was admitted for dehydration and chronic diarrhea. He had been in and out of hospitals with this elusive problem most of his life. When a stool sample showed a laxative, doctors assumed it was a lab error. Mom was too smart and too devoted to make that mistake. Her devotion was especially touching when you saw how little support she had. Her husband never visited once or even called to see how the child was. That was how she explained the child's severe depression. "His father has rejected him. He only loves my younger son," she told the doctors. Brian was that younger son.

A nurse picked up on the fact that little Jesse did smile once in a while, and that was when he was told he'd be having a medical procedure like a shot. That was most unusual of course. Even the sickest child whimpers when they see a needle coming at them. Jesse smiled and looked at his mother for approval. That was the first red flag. The second came when a psychiatric consult was ordered and mom refused it, furiously denouncing the "idiots" who ordered it. Suddenly the laxative in the stool sample was beginning to make sense. Unfortunately, Jesse was dead less than twenty-four hours later.

Anyone who wasn't convinced yet saw the light when mom couldn't stay away from the hospital after the baby died. She came back to visit the nurses over and over again as if the hospital was a place of good memories for her, not bad. When she mentioned that the second child was starting to have diarrhea, everyone realized that little Brian was in danger.

The doctors did all they could do to protect Brian. They notified social services in both states. But they had no proof. And mom had moved soon after, leaving no forwarding address. The tone of the article is one of profound regret that they let Jesse die and might be letting Brian slip through their fingers as well. It is a cautionary tale written early in the understanding of MBP.

"Do you want to know where your brother is buried?" I asked Brian.

"Yeah."

"I haven't seen a headstone more recent than 1950 in this cemetery, so I doubt if he's here, but I could call Janet and find out where he is buried."

"That would be cool," he said.

I called and left messages for weeks. Brian asked every day what I had learned. Finally I called all the local cemeteries and asked if there was anyone buried there by that name and found him. I got directions to the particular plot, and still hadn't heard back from Janet on the subject.

I asked Brian if he had told Dr. Landry about wanting to find his brother. I thought she might be the appropriate person to take him there. He had no interest in that. I was trying to handle this in a way that DHS would find acceptable. And I was trying to get out of it. I have a dead sister myself. The subject was very emotional to me. I broke down in the counselor's office talking about it. I was glad Brian wasn't there.

Finally, there was no more excuse for delay. I had exact directions. I told Brian I had located the gravesite and we decided to go there instead of to the dog park that evening.

We went to the proper intersection within the cemetery. Then we counted four plots east and two north. It was supposed to be there. We didn't see anything so we started over. We spent almost an hour trying to figure out what we could have done wrong and where else it might be before Stephen spotted it. Ginkgo was digging and spread the grass enough to uncover a tiny marker. It had Jesse's first and last name, but no middle name. Under that was the year of his birth and the year of his death, period.

Brian walked over, looked down at the marker and the color drained from his face. He stood and stared, blinking furiously, then suddenly started yelling at the dog to stop digging by it.

"He's not hurting anything," Stephen said, and Brian turned and stomped away.

"He wasn't doing anything," Stephen said to me, defending Ginkgo.

"It's not about the dog. He's just upset."

"He's the one who wanted to see his brother's grave."

"I don't think he expected to feel the way he felt." I don't think he expected it to be so small, I thought.

"Let's go," Brian called over his shoulder as he stomped ahead of us to the car. He got in the back seat and leaned so far out the car window, neither Steve nor I could see his face. I turned the radio up a little, in case he didn't want us to hear what he didn't want us to see. He went straight to his room, not emerging again until the next morning after Stephen left for day camp.

He was himself again, though a little more subdued. He asked if we could go back to the cemetery, this time with flowers. I said yes.

I thought we might talk some about the situation, but Brian wasn't in the mood. He didn't even stay by his brother's grave very long. He just laid the flowers there and walked away. We did stay in the cemetery for a while though, walking from monument to monument, commenting on which ones were pretty, which ones were boring, which looked like someone really cared.

I let Lesley know what I had done. She got the angry phone call from DHS when they got the angry phone call from Brian's family after his weekend visit.

"She didn't have permission to do that," Janet complained to Lesley.

"You could have called her and told her that."

CHAPTER 17

Hysterical
and Over-involved

Brian and I had a project that summer and that was to sell my house. It was something I had thought about for a long time, but in the summer of 2000 everything fell into place. I'd loved my old Victorian when I bought it. It was in a great neighborhood, walking distance from good schools. Tony and Renee had been in middle school when we moved in, so the small yard wasn't an issue. Now that I had foster kids, and some of them young, I wished I had more play space inside and out.

My friend Carol had moved to a small town 45 minutes to the north. The first time I visited, I admitted to her that I was insanely jealous. She had a great big old farmhouse on 85 acres for half what I was paying! To make it even better timing, houses in my neighborhood were selling like hotcakes.

So while Stephen was at camp, Brian and I repaired and decorated and then disappeared so the house could be shown. And when we had a day to ourselves, we drove around Carol's neighborhood and looked at houses for sale. It was fun.

When it was over, Brian was set on one house in particular and I agreed with him. It was a simple three-bedroom ranch surrounded by pine trees. The back yard was fenced and full of playground equipment and even a playhouse. The front yard was a beautiful expanse of lawn punctuated by gardens rolling downhill towards the road. At the far end was a tree with a fort in it. It was kid heaven.

Brian was more impressed with the basement. He thought that was teenager heaven. It was finished and as big as the entire upstairs. The big room was set up with TV, stereo and video games. One small room had a computer and a bed. The other had exercise equipment.

"I want the downstairs to be my bedroom," Brian told everyone.

"I can't very well give you half the house, Brian," I argued.

"Steve can have the backyard. I'm not going to be swinging on swings or playing in the playhouse. It's only fair that I get my own space."

"So Stephen's bedroom will be a tent in the backyard? That's going to be a problem in the winter."

I didn't tell him, but as a foster child, he wasn't allowed to sleep in a basement even if it was teenager heaven. I didn't know it at the time, and wouldn't have told him if I did that, but as a foster child he wasn't allowed to even hang out in the basement, as it had no bulkhead door. There was no need to tell him because he wouldn't be living there with us. Brian was scheduled to move in with his aunt and uncle the first week in September, right before school started. Once my house sold and my offer was accepted on the new house, we had a closing date in late September.

I did the best I could to accept the inevitability of Brian's moving. It wasn't so much that I couldn't part with him. I had parted with Marie and recovered. Tony and Renee had left the nest and, as long as we kept in contact, I was fine with it. My concern for Brian was that this move could be fatal. Everything I read emphasized that. But, short of kidnapping him, there wasn't much I could do.

I decided that I would put my efforts towards getting better acquainted with his aunt and uncle so we could stay in touch after Brian moved in with them. I have to say his Aunt Beth and Uncle Bill seemed like great people and great parents. They would have passed my home study. As I told Lesley I was sure they wouldn't do him any harm on purpose. If they let him see his mother again, it would be out of kindness. And ignorance.

Both the boys went to sleepover camp for a week in July. Steve's camp was just regular kid camp. Brian's was kayaking and rock climbing camp. I took advantage of the time to work every shift possible at a nearby hospital, because as always, money was in short supply.

It was just after the kids got back from camp that I got the word. Brian would be leaving sooner than expected. Instead of September, he would be moving in a week. No reason for the change was given.

I guess I'm guilty of some flip-flopping of my own because in the panic I felt at learning he was going, I found a little more fight in me. In a last minute gesture of desperation, what they call in sports a "Hail Mary" play, I called Laurie, the detective. She and I hadn't talked in months. Technically, she wasn't part of the team, as she was working on the case against Brian's mother and we were supposedly working for Brian. I hadn't sent her the letters I'd sent the others or called her until this point.

But now I thought maybe she had some legal angle that could be used to stop this move, so I called her on the phone and told her the whole sad and frustrating story. She was, thank God, very upset to hear that Brian was going with any member of his family, let alone his mother's family, let alone out-of-state. She thought, like I did, that Brian was making it very clear he didn't feel safe in the situation. She called me back later and said she had a plan.

She set up an appointment with Brian at a place that had a two-way mirror. She was going to ask Brian about the Mother's Day present, about the comments made about his family saying what they had to say to get him, and about the incident with the great grandmother. She said if she could get him to say the same things to her he said to me, with a witness on the other side of the mirror, she might be able to go to the judge with it and get the move stopped.

The meeting happened. I waited in a waiting room while it happened. Brian came out afterwards and told me it was "dumb" and he didn't know why he had to do it. But that was all I heard. Laurie didn't come back out to the waiting room. And she didn't call me at home to say how it went. She didn't return my calls. Brian and I proceeded as if the meeting hadn't happened, and got him ready for his move.

It was a tough time. I knew it would be tough for me, and I knew it would be tough for Steve. But I didn't know how Brian would react. He still verbalized that he wanted to go back home. He still went off happily for weekend visits. He still drove me crazy with his laziness and I drove him crazy with my insistence that he clean his room and pick up his dishes.

But when I told him he was leaving on August 7th, his face just fell. From that point on he spent most of his time lying face down on his bed. I perked him up briefly by getting a couple of kittens for us. I had checked it out with his aunt and uncle and they had agreed that he could bring a kitten with him. So we got a pair of siblings and named them Jesse and Jersey. He took Jersey, as he said his family would not like him naming a cat after his brother. I said, "I'll be the keeper of Jesse for you," and he said okay.

He did absolutely no packing until the night before the move and then he threw everything in garbage bags, and played quietly with Steve and the kittens in his room. I let him take a Benadryl for sleep when he said he knew he would be awake all night. The next morning, he moved down to the living room and lay face down on the couch. I couldn't get him up to eat breakfast.

We said our good-byes before Janet showed up. I didn't want to give her the satisfaction of seeing me cry. He seemed to feel the same way. So we hugged in the house when we saw her pull up then calmly loaded his things into her van.

She chirped, "You must be so excited!" and he grunted, "Yeah." The last I saw of him, he was staring straight ahead, a blank look on his face as the van pulled away.

In spite of the good-bye scene that had taken place in my driveway, I still had hopes that it might not really be the end. You see, the evening before Janet came to pick him up, I'd gotten a most unexpected phone call from my friend Carol.

Unbeknownst to me, she had also gotten in contact with Louise Lasher, the expert on MPB, and had stayed in contact while I had not. She had just talked to her that evening and called me to say Louise didn't think it had to be over. She thought I could still go to the judge myself and get the placement decision reversed.

"You know how you're always saying that Brian has fallen through the cracks so many times?" Carol asked. "Well, don't take this the wrong way, but you're letting it happen again."

I got off the phone feeling like I'd been kicked in the gut and went to join Steve and Brian finding solace with kitties.

After Steve went to bed, I turned to Brian.

"Brian, I got a phone call earlier from Carol. She thinks I can fight and get you moved back here. She's been talking to an expert on your situation, someone from out of state who says I can go to the judge tomorrow with specific information, and they might send you back here. I can call the expert and find out what to do, but I've got to know…do you want me to keep fighting for you?"

To be honest I wanted him to say no. I was emotionally drained. But he said yes. Specifically, he said, "I'd rather Carol did it, because if you do, they might get mad at you and never let me come back."

After he went to bed, I called Louise, then I went to my computer and composed yet another letter. So when Brian drove off with Janet, I may have blinked back a few tears, but I wasn't finished. Instead I ran in the house to change clothes. Fifteen minutes later I was pulling out of the driveway in my best "dress for success" outfit, with a manila envelope full of letters.

I drove all the way to Augusta and no one would even see me. When the judge told me to go away, I went to a legal aid office. When the lawyer told me there was no use fighting DHS, I went to the newspaper. When the editor told me they couldn't print a story due to confidentiality laws, I went to the police station.

I sat across from Laurie feeling completely drained and foolish in my snazzy dress and heels and asked, "What happened? Why didn't you get back to me after you met with Brian?"

She shook her head. "He denied everything. He said there was no Mother's Day present and he was completely confident that his aunt and uncle would keep him from his mother. He said he didn't know why you were saying the things you were saying but that they weren't true."

I was speechless.

"And," she continued, "the judge won't see you because she has already been warned about you by DHS. Everyone has."

"Warned about what?"

"That you're hysterical, over-involved and trying to adopt Brian."

Divide and conquer is a time-honored method of achieving power within a group. Done right, it works extremely well. By the look on Laura's face, by the look on the judge's face, by the tone of the Pediatrician's voice when he told me he was an expert on MPB, I could tell DHS had done it very well.

It seemed Brian had helped them, though. That's the part I couldn't understand. I don't know what he had to gain by playing people against each other. Maybe old habits die hard for him too.

I've received three emails from Brian since he left. There was a silly one telling me to eat frozen spinach. We had an ongoing feud about spinach. I prefer canned. A few months later a short "Hi, How are you guys?" appeared in my Inbox, but no response came to my response. Then last month he wrote that his mother was not convicted and he was going back home.

Every time I hear from him I am reassured that he is still alive.

There is a chapter in the book, *Patient or Pretender,* by Dr. Marc Feldman, titled "Victims of the Great Pretenders." The second paragraph goes as follows:

"Because they are the most directly victimized, the children who are preyed upon through Munchausen by Proxy are the most obvious casualties in the factitious (fake) disorder cases. But there are also many indirect victims: for example, the emotionally drained, guilt-ridden health professionals who unknowingly put children through the torture of unnecessary tests and procedures, and the horrified family members and friends who had unintentionally lent support to an abusive situation. As in MBP cases, every form of factitious disorder leaves victims in its wake. Virtually everyone who comes in contact with the factitious patient becomes a victim of emotional rape to some degree, and the longer and more intense the relationship, the more profound and devastating the experience can be."

When I think back on the five months I had Brian, I think I might have been one of his mother's victims too, like one of the outermost ripples made by a stone thrown in a pond.

Maybe the other team members were victims too.

There are lots of pictures of Brian on the mantel. I don't look at them much because they make me sad.

Amy Lynn

I was watching TV one evening with one of my short-term foster kids, when a sitcom character made a comment about having been in labor for 24 hours.

"Wow!" the little girl exclaimed. Then she turned to me. "Do you know what I would say if I was in labor for that long?"

"What?"

"I would say, 'DHS isn't getting this kid!'"

CHAPTER 18

Her Ideal Mother

A few years back, when my own kids were little, I worked in an ICU at a large medical center. One day I took care of a patient, fresh out of open-heart surgery, who had not done so well. When the doctor was giving me report, as we settled the patient into the unit, he listed the intravenous drugs the man was on to maintain his vital signs. This was early in my tenure as an ICU nurse and the first time I had a patient on so many medications.

"What do I do if his blood pressure continues to drop?" I asked the surgeon.

"Go up on his epinephrine," he answered. That was what I needed to know, which IV drip to play with.

"How high can I go?"

"As high as you need to." There was a mild annoyance in his answers so I knew he thought they were self-evident.

A couple hours later, the epinephrine rate was so high that I had to call the pharmacy to mix a bag with a higher concentration so the patient wouldn't get too much fluid. I was concerned because, while the epinephrine was maintaining a good blood pressure, it was also having the side effect of increasing the heart rate. I called the surgical resident to let him know.

"Okay, thanks," he said after I gave him all the pertinent numbers. I thought he was either coming by to help me come up with a better plan, or he thought things were okay. When he didn't show up, I assumed the latter.

Two hours later, the respiratory therapist did a routine blood gas and discovered that the patient was acidotic. This is also a side effect of epinephrine and it is also dangerous. I called the resident again.

"We'll be there on rounds soon," he said, and I went back to pacing and staring at monitors in the patient's room.

An hour later the team showed up at the desk and I dashed out to tell the surgeon what was going on.

His eyes bulged out of his head and he roared, "The epinephrine is at what?! Did I hear you right?"

I repeated the dose, and then went on to tell him what the heart rate was and the fact that the patient was acidotic.

Needless to say, every other conversation at the desk had stopped by the time he bellowed again, "When were you going to tell someone?"

"I did notify your resident at two and again at four," I said.

"So I am blithely walking around this hospital," he said, swinging his arms mockingly, "thinking everything is okay with my patient, and you're running a goddamn code in here!" He was referring to the Code 99 procedure done for a cardiac arrest, in which epinephrine is given undiluted, straight into the vein.

"I did notify your resident at two and again at four, " I repeated, not because it was the salient point, but because my brain had shut off and all my mouth could do was to repeat the last thing I said.

He turned to the resident and said slowly, enunciating each word, "Apparently, this was not only nursing's error."

The resident turned beet red. "I'm sorry," he said. "This is the first time I've worked with epinephrine. I guess I didn't know that was a significant dose."

I tell this story because it came to my mind a lot after Brian left, when I was trying to remember another time in my life when I felt so bad about my work and myself. Both episodes left me reviewing the details over and over in my mind looking for things I could have done different and finding plenty. Both left me demoralized, feeling like I needed to find a new career, one that didn't involve people.

The difference was that in the ICU, we were able to fix the situation and the patient did fine. We were also able to learn from our mistakes by rehashing the incident until we all saw where our communications broke down. There were no leftover animosities. I knew the surgeon's anger was in defense of his patient, so I didn't hold it against him. We continued to work together, maybe even a better team because of the incident. But we were, for six more years, a team.

I couldn't see how this most recent situation was going to have a positive ending. Brian was in another state where I might never know what happened to him. The team never was a team, so it couldn't become a better one.

I had grown closer to no one for all the pain we went through, except possible Lesley, though I think I put her in career jeopardy at certain points. Carol wasn't speaking to me anymore. She thought I should have kept fighting. I knew I would refuse any child who came from that particular DHS office. I'm sure they felt the same way about me. I wished I could just get out of the business altogether. But I had Steve and I wouldn't do that to him.

I wished I could have just kept Stephen. He came with a great team, something I had come to believe was more important, in terms of the success of the placement, than the child himself. In other words, I could handle any child with the right support. But without support, I didn't even want to try again.

"Next time I'll interview the DHS worker before I agree to take the child, " I told Lesley. Unfortunately, next time had to come quick.

Between getting the house ready for sale, getting the boys ready for camp, making it all up to Stephen with trips to the movies and the arcade, vet bills for the two new pets, I was completely broke. I was making practically nothing selling the house, thanks to a second mortgage, and what I was making would be needed as a down payment on the next house. I couldn't even afford to get an inspection done on the new house, the numbers were so tight.

And here I was, effectively on half salary, with only one child. "I can't afford to lick my wounds more than two weeks," I told Lesley. "Then I have to get back to work."

"We don't think it would be a good idea to place another child with you so soon," she said.

"Oh?"

"With the move and all."

"I know it's bad timing." I said. "I thought Brian would be here another month. But if we get someone soon enough, they can get to know Steve and me, visit the new house with us, pick their own bedroom. We can make it fun."

I could tell this was hard for her. "We don't think we can place a child until you are settled in for a while."

"How do we think I'm going to pay my bills until that happens?" I asked.

"Maybe you could make an appointment with Marguerite and get permission to work more than 15 hours a week."

I'll be damned if I'll ask permission to get out of a corner you've backed me into, I thought to myself. "The extra hours don't become magically available just because I need them," I said.

"I don't know what to tell you," she answered.

The discussion continued later with Karen, as I wasn't satisfied with Lesley's explanation. She kept referring to "agency policy" that didn't allow children to be placed within a month on either side of a move.

"These kids tend to have moved a lot already so it is traumatic for them."

"Unless moving a lot means they are used to it."

"Some maybe."

"But you don't have any of them waiting for foster homes?"

"It's agency policy."

"So basically, you're telling me that all the children out there waiting for homes would be better off where they are now than with me. They may not have me to come to when this is over." I threatened.

"I realize we may be losing a good foster home over this…"

I couldn't help but wonder if that was the point. Private agencies are dependent on DHS for referrals. If DHS was angry enough with me, they could take it out on the agency, holding back referrals. I would have no way of knowing if that was happening.

Work was my only option and I was already working more than I was supposed to. I'd kept it under 15 hours a week, but I did it all while the boys were at respite, which is a licensing violation.

Respite is a fancy name for baby-sitting. Treatment level foster parents get a limited number of respite days a year. With that I was able to send the boys to Darlene, our respite worker's house every other weekend, and pull two twelve-hour shifts in the ER while they were gone. DHS dictates that half of all respite days have to be used for recreation, not work. I justified it by having a really good time while I was at work.

Now I was going to have to have a really good time at work while Stephen was at day camp too. Even with that, I borrowed $500 from each of three credit cards just to get by until Amy Lynn moved in.

By the time I was considered "settled" enough to take another child, I was in no position to be picky. If they had said that her DHS worker was the same one I had worked with the last time, I would have had to make some monumental decisions. But they didn't and I didn't. And Amy Lynn's worker turned out to be one of the most delightful people I've met in this business.

Laurel and I hit it off immediately. It might have helped that she was close to my age, divorced, and had college age kids, but it also helped that she had a sense of humor. In just one phone conversation I knew we would get along, so I was willing to take my chances with Amy Lynn.

Amy Lynn was also a pleasant surprise…at first. She was nine, an attractive child, the kind of child phrases like "cute as a button" were made for. She had big round eyes and brown hair that hung like a silk blanket on either side of her face. She was nervous the day we met her in her old foster home but not shy. The minute Steve and I walked in the front door she popped out of her seat and started to chatter.

"Am I moving in with you? Because I could, you know, if it's okay. I used to be bad, but I'm better now…" The lisp was adorable.

"Let's just spend the day together first, okay? Let's see if you like our house."

Amy Lynn spent the afternoon making our backyard playhouse into her own. Controlling little thing that she was, she had every kid in the neighborhood helping her decorate, hanging pictures on the wall and moving plastic furniture. I only saw her when it was time to eat, and then she carried the conversation, telling us about her past and why she was in foster care.

Her version of the story had to do with her mother being too young, with too many kids, and the state thinking the older kids had too much responsibility for the younger ones. I didn't have to comment. Between her stories and Steve's competing detail about his own life, I only had to "ooh" and "ah" occasionally.

"My mom was sixteen when she had me."

"Well my mom was fourteen when she had my brother."

The "get acquainted" day would have been perfect (or "perthect" as Amy Lynn said) if her foster mother had been home at six when I brought Amy Lynn back. But she was not. Stephen and I had planned to rent a movie after dropping Amy off, but now it only made sense to go to Home Vision Video and then try to drop Amy off again.

I had a gut feeling this would not be a simple errand. Amy had already made it clear she liked to be the center of attention. Steve would be the center of attention picking out this movie. I was interested in seeing how Amy handled that.

As we walked up and down the aisles at Home Vision, I took note of Amy's body language. Her breathing speeded up slightly as she registered the fact that this was not about her. Her head tilted back and her jaw clenched as she watched Stephen make a choice for the evening's entertainment. As we approached the cash register, she saw a bin full of key chains and grabbed one with a sigh of relief.

"I'll need a key chain for the new house," she announced. "You can buy me this one."

"You won't need a key, Amy Lynn." I said. "You won't be coming home to an empty house."

She wasn't crazy about that explanation. "But I collect key chains and I don't have this one," she said, laying it on the counter for me to purchase.

I knew this would be a telling moment. "Not today, Amy Lynn. We're just here for the movie."

She slammed the key chain back in the bin and shot to the back of the store. I could see her little head moving back and forth as she paced angrily. My heart raced a little too while I wondered what she was capable of when she didn't get her way. The memory of Tina in the parking lot was still fresh in my mind. I didn't relish a scene, but I knew now was the time to have one if we were going to. Now it was essential I make clear that I was in charge. On the surface I remained calm and matter of fact.

"Let's go, Amy," I called, as Stephen and I headed for the door. She hesitated, then came running out, red faced and tearful, and climbed into the back seat.

I pulled out of the parking lot. She stared out the window. Stephen waited, instinctively knowing something was coming.

All of a sudden Amy Lynn bounced in her seat and smiled. "I think I just found my ideal mother!" she said.

Five months later, when Amy Lynn left, she handed me a note that said I was "the gret fostemom."

In between, she called me every name in the book.

✦ ✦ ✦

CHAPTER 19

Fat, Dumb and Ugly

Amy Lynn was a master of the temper tantrum. If it was an Olympic sport, she would get high marks for technique, but slightly lower for presentation. The effort always showed a little too much.

Like the time we were ordering food at Arby's… Amy Lynn wanted mozzarella cheese sticks as well as curly fries with her sandwich. I said no, that she had to pick one or the other. Her tantrum warm-up began with grumbling and shuffling, and then she tried another angle.

"I'll skip the sandwich and just have the fries and cheese sticks," she announced, while the counter girl and the patrons behind us waited.

"That's not what I'm offering." I told her, "You can have a sandwich and a side dish. If you want both side dishes, maybe you can order one and Stephen can order the other and you two can share."

"That's not fair!" she yelled at the top of her lungs. "Why do I always have to share with Stephen? Stephen gets anything he wants and I don't get anything! You hate me because I'm a foster child! You think I'm a fat, dumb, ugly foster child!"

It was almost funny. The whole restaurant was suddenly facing our direction. Part of me wanted to clarify that Stephen was also a foster child, and she was not being denied food. Part of me wanted to put my hand over her mouth and drag her out to the car. But decisions have to be made quickly at moments like that and mine was to just go on as if she wasn't yelling, showing her that she didn't scare me. So I turned away from her, shrugged at the counter girl and completed our order. Amy Lynn soon discovered that she could only say so many times that she was a poor, mistreated foster child and when no one responded, she quieted down and followed us to a table in the back. She looked a little confused when she sat down with us and waited to see what I was going to do.

"We have cheese sticks and curly fries." I said. "Since Amy Lynn behaved badly, Stephen gets to pick. He can have either one, or he can choose to share both with Amy Lynn."

He chose to share.

"See how easy that was," I said. Sometimes I think letting them twist in the wind and wonder about the consequences is punishment itself and one I rather enjoy.

I didn't bring up her tantrum again until we got home and I told her she would be going straight to bed for her "abominable" behavior. She accepted it.

During her goodnight hug and kiss I made a suggestion. "Next time, you ought to try throwing yourself on the floor." I told her.

"What?"

"For a really effective temper tantrum, you need to throw yourself to the ground and kick. Pounding on the floor is a nice touch too. Want to try it?"

She smiled slowly. Stephen was getting the joke too.

"I'll show you," he offered.

"No, I will," I said. "Or we can all do it. Shall we? Let's all throw ourselves on the ground and kick and scream."

They took me up on it and for a minute it was all fun and games. But I stopped it quickly and made sure she knew she was still punished even if I did tease her about it. She still had to go to bed early.

"There won't be a next time, will there?" I asked as I tucked her in. She gave the right answer and I patted myself on the back for a job well done. Prematurely, it turns out. Very prematurely.

Amy Lynn was to throw a good number of temper tantrums, but she never flung herself to the ground as I suggested. It would have interfered with the verbal tirade. People might not have understood clearly that she was a foster child, a fat dumb and ugly one at that, if she was yelling it into the linoleum.

I was the one who was fat, dumb and ugly during one tantrum. That was the one she threw during her social worker Laurel's visit. I don't even remember what she was mad about that time. But she was mad! Stephen and I went outside to shoot baskets while she pled her case to Laurel about being moved to a better foster home. A couple of neighbor boys came over to play with us, but when they heard the words flying out of our dining room window, they stopped and listened, jaws hanging.

I always tried to stay cool on the outside, but in truth, I was sweating inside, hoping no one was actually believing Amy Lynn. I knew Laurel well enough that I thought I could count on that. But I still felt I needed to handle it just right, to keep Laurel from suspecting Amy Lynn may have some valid complaints.

Finally, I decided to go back in the house and join the conversation. I grabbed the mail from the mailbox on my way in and I immediately knew I had hit pay dirt. There was a Delia's catalogue on the top of the pile. Amy Lynn loved the clothes in the Delia's catalogue.

I sat down at the dining room table and laid the stack of mail down in front of me with a thud. Amy Lynn stopped yelling mid-sentence. She walked over to the table and started flipping through the pages looking at tank tops on skinny little models.

Then she looked up at me. "I need some new clothes, you know," she said sweetly.

"That's true," I answered.

"Can we order some from here?" she asked sliding onto my lap.

"Maybe."

She leaned back and kissed me on the cheek.

Laurel shook her head in disbelief. I smiled at her over Amy Lynn's shoulder.

One little catalogue changed the balance of power completely. Amy now had more to gain by buttering me up than by getting sympathy from her social worker, so Laurel might as well have just slipped out quietly, as far as Amy was concerned. She wasn't needed any more. Amy and I continued to flip through the pages, admiring sparkling jeans, tee shirts and hair bows. Laurel finally spoke up.

"So, Amy Lynn, I need to go now," she said. "You okay?"

Amy Lynn smiled.

"You don't want me to find a new foster home for you after all?"

"No," she said sweetly. "I love it here."

And with that, another episode of high drama was over. By then I knew better than to think it would be the last.

CHAPTER 20

Tryin' to Stop Lyin'

Tantrums are unpleasant, but they are not the scariest thing to a foster parent. False allegations are. Amy Lynn bordered on that during her tantrums. I tried to remind her later when she was calm, that it was wrong to say I treated Stephen better than her because he wasn't a foster child. He *was* a foster child.

"Yeah, I know," she'd say.

"Do you just say it because it gets people's attention?"

"Yeah."

"You're going to get yourself in big trouble doing that some day," I told her.

"I know," she told me. "I've been lying my whole life. I'm trying to learn how to stop."

"You know how you stop?"

"How?"

"Just stop. No more lies. I'm going to remind you next time I think you're lying, okay?"

She thought that was okay. She even took it well when I reminded her, as long as it wasn't me she was mad at and lying about. When she told me that she'd been raped "about a zillion times" I asked a few questions about when and by whom. When the answers were completely implausible (by a man who climbed in her windows at night and left notes on her pillow telling her what he did), I asked, "Is that true?"

She pounded the table with her fist and said, "Darn!"

"What's the matter?"

"I'm trying to stop that lying."

"So you weren't raped?"

"No."

"Do you even know what rape is?"

"No."

When she told me her former foster mother made her eat leftover macaroni and cheese instead of turkey on Thanksgiving, I asked. "Did you even live with her during the holidays? I thought you moved there in January."

She stomped her foot. "Lying again," she told me.

"Someday you're going to tell a lie and get yourself in all kinds of trouble," I warned her. But it was really myself I was worried about. She still told lies about me when she was angry.

Once she told my next-door neighbor that I kept her locked in the basement and that I only fed Stephen. When Linda called to let me know, she said, "You've got to get rid of that girl. She had me believing it for a while. She's so convincing."

I called the school the next day and asked if she had told any stories there. "Oh, of course," her teacher said. "Locked in the basement, never fed, she said that about her last foster mother too."

Thank goodness she'd stayed in the same school with the move and I didn't have to convince a new group of people.

"You know our basement is a big playroom with a TV and video games in it." I said "If I was going to punish her I would lock her out of there, not in," I said. "Anyway, there is no lock on the door."

"Don't worry. We know her," the teacher reassured me. "But she did tell me you hate me the other day."

"What!?"

"She didn't like being told what to do and she said, 'I told my foster mother how you are and she said she hates you.'"

I was mortified. "I hope you know…"

"Don't worry. We know Amy Lynn."

I had told myself very early in the foster care experience that I wouldn't take any chances with a child who made up lies. The idea of ending up charged with some kind of abuse was a nightmare, but an even worse nightmare was having my biological kids accused. I would never forgive myself if my son Tony got accused of a crime just because I chose to keep a child who made false allegations. When the subject comes up in foster parent training we are told that false allegations are so common that there is a hotline for foster parents to call, as well as support groups for the accused to attend while waiting for the outcome. I did not find that comforting. I didn't want Tony attending support groups because of my mistake in judgment.

Now I was getting nervous. If I was going to stick to my convictions, then Amy Lynn had to go. All of my friends agreed that they wouldn't take the chance I was taking. But they didn't live with her. They didn't cuddle with her every evening while watching *Friends* and have long talks about life. They didn't love her and love a challenge the way I did.

Besides, she was on the reunification track. The goal was that she would be back with her mother and four siblings within the year. She had already been in three foster homes. I didn't want to make it four. I called Lesley to brainstorm.

Lesley was not only reassuring but also logical. She pointed out that, while she knew any accusations of abuse would be false, she was not the only member of the team. I needed to touch base with the others, and see what kind of support I felt I had. The core team included Amy's guardian *ad litem*, her counselor and her DHS worker.

There were also peripheral team members who could stir up trouble if they believed one of Amy Lynn's stories.

Her teachers had already reassured me. I hoped they would communicate with the bus driver. There was a DHS driver who took her to see her mother every Saturday. And there was her mother.

I liked Amy Lynn's mother from the moment I met her. She had come to the house once for a visit and I had seen her at team meetings. She was sweet and pretty and way too young to have so many kids by different fathers. She lost custody when someone reported that she left the older ones to care for the younger ones when she went out on dates with even more prospective fathers. Supposedly, she once locked them all in a cold basement, so DHS wouldn't be able to find them unsupervised, then didn't return for two days.

I had been told that story by the former foster mother, and believed it because I saw no reason not to believe it. When I dialed mom's phone number after talking to Lesley, I wondered, could that story have come from Amy Lynn? Would she have made something so awful up about the mother she claimed to love and miss so much?

"How do you think I got in this mess?" was mom's response when I told her that Amy Lynn was telling lies about me. It hit me hard. Here I was worried about my reputation, my income and other relatively minor concerns. This woman had lost her family. She was allowed to keep the baby with her, but the other four children were scattered in different foster homes. DHS was bargaining with her as to which ones they would give back and which ones they wanted to put up for adoption. She had already signed away her oldest and was profoundly depressed afterwards. DHS was hesitating to send back any more kids while she was depressed and hinting that she needed to give up one or two more before they would return the rest. What if this was all the result of one of Amy Lynn's fabrications?

I felt better only for myself after my conversation with Amy Lynn's mother. I knew she would not believe one of her daughter's stories. And the driver? She was a gray-haired old woman who confided in me once that her own grandchildren were in foster care, about to be released for adoption. She frankly hated DHS because they would not consider placing the kids with her, but she drove for them in hopes of running into the grandchildren somewhere along the way. She wasn't likely to turn on me.

I left messages on voice mails for the rest of the team. I wouldn't have been worried about the DHS worker if it was still Laurel. Unfortunately, she had resigned shortly after her last visit to our home. She swore it wasn't the tantrum that drove her off but another job that beckoned.

The new worker's name was Pat Gibson and my contact with her had been minimal and unpleasant. She didn't make eye contact when I was introduced to her at a team meeting. Later when I asked where the bathroom was she ignored me. Lesley was there and witnessed it all. We commiserated on the phone later about our new leader. Now I had to report that Amy Lynn was telling others that I abused her. I left the message on Friday afternoon.

Amy Lynn's stories were not the only concern I wanted to discuss with her new DHS worker and this was not the first message I'd left. In the weeks since she took over, we had developed a pattern. I would leave a long message with detailed information and questions as well as times I would be available to talk on the phone. She would call back at the one time that I'd said I wouldn't be home and leave an equally long message, sometimes responding to my concerns and sometimes not.

Issues we had discussed by phone tag included Amy Lynn's visits with her mom. The visits themselves were not the problem. It was the rides. Someone else in the DHS office made the arrangements and would call to inform me of the times of departure and arrival. Somehow, they were always wrong. Once I was told the ride was coming at 9 A.M. and they showed up at 4 P.M. That was not an easy day for Amy Lynn. The most recent debacle had the driver bringing her home an hour early and finding an empty house. Without so much as leaving me a note, he (new driver) took her to a different foster home, and left her there. The foster dad was the one home at the time, assumed his wife had agreed to this, and didn't try to find me. When his wife got home three hours later I finally learned where Amy Lynn was. That was not a bad day for Amy Lynn, but a frantic one for me. I left a message on Pat's voice mail.

Another issue was Amy Lynn's counselor. When I first met her, I thought it was okay that she was a little bizarre. I told Lesley I felt like we were seeing Psychic Sue from the *Will and Grace* TV show. She had long henna-dyed hair and bare feet, wore flowing hippie skirts and showed us her tattoos. She brought her dog to work with her. I thought her cartoonish qualities might help her connect with kids, so that alone did not bother me.

The fact that Stephen and I had to wait in an empty closet sitting on pillows didn't even bother me. It was the things I heard her say to Amy that led me to express my concerns to Laurel first and then to her replacement Pat. *anything can happen*

By this time, I didn't know what to expect from a counselor any more than I knew what to expect from a social worker or a guardian *ad litem*. Each one seemed to read from a different rulebook. But I knew, no matter how she operated, the counselor had a lot of power. She would be reporting to the DHS worker about Amy's adjustment to the placement.

I had most recently dealt with Brian's psychiatrist who wanted no dialogue with me at all, and Stephen's counselor who only wanted a brief "check in" if there were behavior problems at home. Marie's counselor never spoke to me at all except to set up future appointments. I was prepared to spend this hour in the waiting room/closet with Stephen, but Theresa Jo called me in. Without any warning she proceeded to tell Amy Lynn how to run my life.

"If you have nightmares, Amy Lynn, what are you going to do?" she asked.

"Wake up Mary."

"She doesn't have nightmares." I said, as a sinking feeling in my stomach told me she would now. Theresa Jo ignored me.

"Right. And if you are afraid to go in the basement, what do you do?"

"Tell Mary and she will go down with me."

"Right."

I shook my head, trying to signal the therapist that this was not a good direction to be going, but to no avail. The list continued.

Of course, Amy Lynn's nightmares and other fears began that day. When I told her no one has nightmares five minutes after they go to bed, she stomped back to her room angrily, waited a half hour and came back out claiming now she really did have a nightmare.

But that was Amy Lynn. She was incredibly manipulative, but just as incredibly transparent about it. When she did something wrong and was afraid of the consequences she would coo, "Pretty mommy, pretty mommy."

When she wanted to get Stephen's goat, she would call him a name, get sent to her room and then come right back out again apologizing profusely...to me.

"I thought about what you said," she would tell me, "and I know I was wrong. I'm sorry. Can I have a hug?" Then from my arms, she would shoot a look back over her shoulder at Stephen that said *gotcha!*

Unfortunately for her, I saw the look and made her apologize to Stephen, not to me. That drove her crazy.

When she called me pretty mommy, I said, "Oh for heaven's sake, Amy Lynn, did your other foster mothers fall for that?"

It was often a battle of the wills between Amy Lynn and I, and her therapist had just given her a few more weapons.

The next week I asked Theresa Jo if I could speak to her before the session.

"Please don't bring up problems with Amy Lynn that haven't happened yet." I pleaded. "She is very suggestible. Since last week, she has started having nightmares and fears that she didn't have before. If you could ask me first…" It was hard to maintain any authority when I had to lean around Theresa Jo's big black dog just to see who I was talking to.

Theresa Jo didn't have the same problem. The dog wasn't on her lap. He was on mine. She pulled herself up tall in her chair before she answered me.

"Well," she said, "I think we have some boundary issues here and they aren't with Amy Lynn. I am not accustomed to having therapy dictated by the foster parent."

That conversation went nowhere and soon I was back on the floor of the little closet with Stephen. But she wasn't done with me yet. At the end of the session, Theresa Jo came out and said that I was needed back in her office.

"Amy Lynn has something to say," she practically whispered. "This isn't easy for her. She's been practicing, so go easy on her."

I knew I was headed for the proverbial hot seat.

"I need more attention," Amy Lynn said as soon as I sat down.

Not hitting the counselor at that moment took even more self-control than not strangling Amy Lynn during one of her public tantrums.

"How much attention do you get now?" I asked.

She didn't know how to answer.

"You sit on my lap during *Friends* every night. We work on your reading together after school and I tell you a story at bedtime, right?"

"Right."

"That's about enough. Stephen deserves some attention. And I need time to myself."

Theresa Jo looked at Amy Lynn as if to say, "I'm sorry it went badly honey."

"We're done," I said to Theresa Jo and I took Amy Lynn by the hand and left.

When I said we were done, I meant forever and ever, but Laurel talked me into giving it another try.

"She is a little too attached to Amy Lynn," Laurel admitted. "She has said she'd like to adopt her."

That shocked me "Don't you think that's a problem?" I asked. "How objective can she be? She's going to be reporting to the judge on whether the child should go home again and she wants to adopt her?"

"I know. But we don't have a lot of options. Not many counselors will take foster kids because the pay is so low."

"So they are either the worst therapists around or the most generous."

"Right."

"But either way, they have the ear of the judge. What they say may determine a child's future, whether they go back with their family or stay in foster care."

"Right."

"That doesn't bother you?"

"Why do you think I'm getting out of this business?"

I agreed to give it one more try, only out of respect for Laurel. After a lengthy phone conversation, during which Theresa Jo said things like, "I guess this is what happens when two powerful women come together." and "I think it is good for Amy Lynn to see two powerful women work out their differences." I took Amy back. Not because I fell for any of that, but because I felt I had no choice.

I decided to avoid conflict by just dropping Amy Lynn off and picking her up. I even brought our dog, Ginkgo, so the barking and snarling of the dogs would eliminate the possibility of barking and snarling between us powerful women. I thought that was pretty clever.

The next day Amy Lynn said to me, "My counselor sure hates you. She says you hate her too and you might never bring me back again if I tell you that she told me."

With that, I left a message on the new DHS worker's voice mail. As she never returned my call, I also sent a detailed letter on why I was not going to continue with this therapist.

Then I waited to hear back on all three issues. They were:

1. Problems with the therapist,

2. Problems with the Saturday driving arrangements, and

3. Problems with Amy Lynn's lying.

✦ ✦ ✦

CHAPTER 21

Throwing in the Towel

As difficult as she was and as frustrated as I got with her, I still had a sense there was real promise in Amy Lynn. She was getting better. She was having fewer tantrums, asking for what she needed directly instead of manipulating at least some of the time, and admitting she was jealous of Stephen because she was so used to being jealous of the other kids in her birth home. A lot of things were getting better. Her schoolwork was not.

Amy Lynn was nine years old and couldn't read. Her last foster mother worked very hard with her on it. She had a private tutor the whole summer before I got her. I bought word magnets for the front of the refrigerator and tried to make sentences with her every day. None of us made any headway.

Darlene, our respite worker who had become a close friend, questioned it once. She ran a day care center and was very tuned in to children.

"It looked to me like she was reading the menu on the wall when we were ordering pizza last night," she told me. "I thought you said she couldn't read."

"She can't," I answered, not getting the point she was making. "Maybe she was trying to find words she could read."

I missed it that time, but finally saw it when it was right in front of my nose. We were sitting at the kitchen table eating Kentucky Fried

Chicken, and Amy Lynn announced, "We do chicken right!" looking directly at the words on the side of the box.

"Where do you see that?" I asked.

"Oh," she said, surprised, "I know that's what it says. That's what it always says."

But it was too late. I knew.

I thought long and hard about how to handle my newfound knowledge that Amy Lynn was faking. I knew her well enough to know confronting her would just make her dig her heels in deeper. I was still thinking and brainstorming with the team members who were sane and did return my calls, when a stroke of genius came to me. We were in a toy store killing time while Stephen was at Martial Arts. Amy Lynn was practically hyperventilating over Barbie Dolls. Christmas was coming.

"I wish I could get you one of those for Christmas," I said sadly, "but until you're reading I think we have to stick to things that will help you with that, like computer programs and books."

She was upset, but her wheels were still turning. "Can't I get both?"

"Oh, Honey, computer programs are expensive. There's one in particular we might all go together on because it's so expensive. There won't be any money left over for things like Barbie dolls." I could be manipulative myself when it served a purpose.

Before the day was over, Amy Lynn was putting words together on the front of the refrigerator. Soon she started reading Level I books. I made her read to herself before going to sleep then tell me the story at breakfast. I wanted her to get the attention she craved from her ability to read instead of the lack of it. Soon she was done with all the Level II. Her teachers were amazed at her progress. I was amazed at how easy she was to trick.

By Christmas there was no need for computer programs. She was reading like a champ. I was proud of myself, but hurting at the same time. I had given notice on Amy Lynn by then and she was soon to be moved to another foster home. She didn't know it yet.

I was absolutely guilt-ridden by Christmas. Amy Lynn was doing so well. Her attachment to us was beginning to feel sincere. I was getting along with her mother and felt I could help with the transition back home, or if worse came to worse and Amy was chosen as one of the children not to go home, I could help her through it. If only I hadn't given notice. I kept telling myself the story over and over again to remind myself I had no choice. Maybe someone else wouldn't have given notice, but being me, I had no choice.

I'd waited a week to hear back from Pat, the DHS worker. I had left a clear message about when I would be at home and, of course, she called back when she knew I wouldn't. I had also been clear about what my concerns were, the drivers, the counselor and Amy's lying. I had followed up with a letter. It was late Friday, after a 12 hours shift in the Emergency Room, when I pressed the Play button and heard Pat's droning voice. She did not respond to the issue of Amy's lying at all. Instead, she accused me of lying.

"I spoke to the driver and apparently you're the one who wasn't home when you were supposed to be. I don't appreciate being misled and I'm going to get to the bottom of this. Starting next week, you can transport Amy Lynn to see her mother. That's what you get paid for. Oh, and I've spoken to my supervisor, and we're not ready to give up on the therapist. Amy Lynn will continue to see her every Thursday."

I was practically dizzy with rage. Even now my teeth clench as I think of it. I couldn't sleep that night. I wished it wasn't the weekend because I wanted to talk to Lesley about it. On the other hand, the weekend gave me time to cool down before I made a decision that was too hasty. Only I didn't cool down. I was just as angry on Monday morning as I had been on Friday night. But at least the kids were at school, so I didn't have to pretend to be cheery. I called Lesley the moment Agency B opened.

"That woman hates my guts!" I said, "and we have barely ever had a conversation. From the first time I met her she has treated me with utter disrespect. Worse than that. Contempt! Like I am somehow the enemy."

"Unfortunately, some workers feel that way about treatment level foster parents."

"Yeah, I know. I've heard the 'overpaid whores' line. You know, if Amy Lynn was anything but a child…if she were a pet or a houseplant or something, she would be sitting on that woman's desk right now. It's like they've got us by the balls. They can treat us anyway they want to and we won't throw in the towel because we don't want to hurt the child."

"What are you going to do?"

"Throw in the towel."

"Really?"

"Don't worry. I won't leave Amy Lynn on her doorstep. I'll give a month's notice. What choice do I have?"

"To be honest with you…none."

"I have said from the beginning I would not take a child who made false accusations. Then I amended it to be unless I have support of the whole team. Even that I did so I could justify keeping Amy Lynn. But with outright hostility from the team leader, and a counselor who is a nut case…I mean this is a recipe for disaster. This can go nowhere but down."

We decided that I would call the worker, but knowing she wouldn't take my call, Lesley would follow up to make sure she really got the message. Hedging my bets a little I left on her voice mail that I would not be taking Amy Lynn to the counselor, I would not be transporting her to see her mother and if that was a problem, she could take this as my 30-day's notice to remove Amy Lynn. That way the door was left open for that fantasy phone call, the one with the apology and offer to do anything to improve the situation.

Pat did not return my phone call. That turned out to be our last communication for months. She did speak to Lesley and said she would be removing Amy Lynn. That was in mid November.

By the time school started again after Christmas vacation, I had a child who was no longer having tantrums, was working hard to stop lying and was reading. She and Steve were getting along. I looked forward to our little talks during *Friends* every evening.

But there was always that lump in the pit of my stomach. Any day now I expected Pat Gibson to pull up in my driveway and take her. She would feel so betrayed. I didn't know what to do.

Lesley and I talked all the time. "Have you heard anything?"

"No, have you?"

"No. How long has it been?"

"Seven weeks. She hasn't even called to ask if I would keep her longer. Technically, I could just bring her down to DHS and say, 'Times up.'"

"You must be getting so frustrated."

"Yes and no. I'm glad she's still here. I'm dreading her leaving. But I still can't see any other way. I can't work with this team."

"I know you need support because of Amy and her stories, but hasn't she stopped that?"

"Not entirely. She told the kid next door that I only feed her bread and water. He went home and told his mother who called me."

"Oh, my God! What did Amy say?"

"The usual. 'I'm trying to stop lying.' When I took her to the doctor for her Hepatitis B shot, she screamed 'You hate me because I'm a foster child' again. She's better, but not enough to go on with an unsupportive team."

"I can't believe they are dragging this on so long. I can't get anyone to return my calls either."

Later Lesley called back with one more idea. "Have you talked to the guardian *ad litem?*"

I had not. It hadn't even occurred to me. My only contact with him had been an introduction at a team meeting. He was friendly that day. Maybe there was a glimmer of hope.

What I hoped for was that he could wield some power and get that DHS worker replaced by someone I could count on and then Amy Lynn could stay. I wasn't sure he had that much power, or if he did, would care to use it that way. It was unlikely, particularly since Amy Lynn's case involved all her siblings, and it was intended to end soon with reunification. Replacing me was probably easier than replacing Pat Gibson. But, I would give it a shot.

Unfortunately, he was not terribly sympathetic. He was business-like. He took down the information, the date I had given notice, the date of my last contact with DHS. Then asked, "When did the worker visit Amy Lynn last?"

"She has never visited Amy Lynn. She has never even met her."

"What!"

"She has only met me once, that same day you did at the Team meeting. But she has never been out to the house or even talked to Amy on the phone."

That he was angry about. Looking back with logic, it must be said that he had never been to our home either, and had never called Amy or me on the phone. Like DHS, he was mandated to make a visit every three months and had not in the five months Amy was with me. But he sounded angry by the time we hung up the phone and I sensed he was going to do something, though not necessarily what I wanted him to do.

Just two days later I got my first phone call from Pat Gibson in seven weeks. Very pleasantly she said that she needed to make a home visit and asked when a good time would be. She was off the phone so quickly I didn't get a chance to ask her if she had found a new placement for Amy Lynn, if she was going to discuss it with Amy Lynn on the visit or anything for that matter. All I got was a date and time.

The next Thursday at three, she showed up. The three of us sat at the kitchen table for a few minutes. Conversation was light. Amy Lynn bragged about how well she was doing in school. We gave lots of positive reinforcement. Then I suggested that Amy Lynn show Pat her bedroom, sensing that the real conversation would begin when they were alone. So off they went.

Pat was still polite when they emerged an hour later. She said that she and Amy had had a good talk, that Amy Lynn told her what she liked about living with us, and what she didn't. She said she would get back to me. And then she left.

But she didn't get back to me. We were back in Limbo.

✦ ✦ ✦

CHAPTER 22

Retaliation

The wait was frustrating for practical reasons as well as emotional ones. I had found a solution to the problem that Agency B presented when they wouldn't allow me to work more than 15 hours a week, but I couldn't avail myself of it until this issue was resolved. When I had met Laurel, all the way back in October, she told me about another private foster care agency that had a completely different philosophy on work. They actually encouraged parents to have outside work, claimed they would find and pay the baby-sitter. I interviewed with that agency, jumped through all the hoops they wanted me to jump through, and was ready to make the move. All I still needed was a letter from Pat Gibson approving the move or for Amy Lynn to be gone, so I was no longer connected to Pat Gibson. Of course, that was in Limbo too.

The truth is, I was already working 24 hours a week at the Emergency Room at St. Mary's Hospital. I had a wonderful baby-sitter whom I was paying myself. It was tough telling Lesley that we were leaving, but the alternative was staying and trying to hide the fact that I was working. I sensed that she knew and had adopted a "don't ask, don't tell" philosophy because the subject never came up. I was prepared to lie if I had to, but I never did.

Telling Lesley and Agency B that we were jumping ship was an entirely different experience than telling Agency A had been. They said they understood; they knew that I needed the health insurance as well as a way to earn a living when I only had one foster child. Lesley and her superiors did everything they could do to facilitate the move without a single guilt trip laid on me. Of course, considering the trouble I had stirred up with DHS over Brian and the disagreements we had over the years, they may have been jumping for joy that I was leaving.

I always wonder if I am the biggest problem foster parent around or if I am just an average amount of trouble. You'd think I would know from my big network of foster parent friends, but I don't have one. There are support groups at every agency, but they are monitored by the agency social workers, often even run by social workers. We are cautioned not to talk about specifics of each case because it is a violation of confidentiality laws.

So support groups are not really supportive. I only got to be friends with Carol because we both got so annoyed at a support group meeting once that we left in the middle of it and decided in the elevator to go out to breakfast and be our own support group. It turned out to be a lifesaver for me to have her for the year or so we were friends, before the falling out over Brian.

Lesley and I continued to talk regularly on the phone over the winter. I let her be the one to leave messages for Pat Gibson, both about Amy Lynn's placement and about the letter I needed to approve my move. Then one afternoon, three weeks after the home visit, Lesley called. Her voice was trembling. She said she really hated to tell me what she had to tell me.

"I just got off the phone with Lewiston DHS," she said. "I spoke to Pat Gibson as well as her supervisor. They are not going to write a letter of recommendation. They are filing an abuse complaint against you instead."

"For what?"

"They wouldn't say. At first they said it was because you hadn't taken Amy Lynn to counseling. I pointed out that I have documentation of the letters and phone calls on the subject and that you had done everything by the books on that. A few minutes later they called back and said they still think they can make a case for emotional abuse."

"They still think they can make a case for emotional abuse?" I repeated. "That sounds so...I don't know...calculated. Like they are looking for a reason."

"Exactly."

"Like retaliation, pure and simple."

"It does sound that way."

We talked at length and Lesley commented more than once that I was taking it better than she expected. That's where being a critical care nurse comes in handy. Controlling emotion is a job skill I had learned ages ago. Actually, the worse things get the calmer I get.

"I'm doing better than you are." I said. "You sound like you're going to cry."

"Well, they weren't too easy on me either."

"What do you mean?"

"Oh, they said this agency wasn't supervising well enough, that we allowed the abuse to go on."

That pissed me off. Lesley was very competent, but young enough that her confidence could still be shaken easily.

"What abuse?" I asked. "They are telling you that you missed something, buy they won't tell you what. They are saying that I abuse her, but they haven't told me what to stop doing. Do they even realize Amy Lynn is still here?"

"That's what I wanted to talk to you about. They know she's there. Apparently it's not enough abuse to remove her. But it seems logical to me to give them an ultimatum. If you're okay with it, I want to tell them either they drop the complaint or take Amy Lynn now."

"How about giving them ten days?"

And that's what Lesley did. Pat Gibson responded that they would have a placement in ten days.

When the kids got home, I was still in shock, which looks a lot like calm. It was actually a good state to be in at that moment. I didn't want the kids to think I was falling apart, even if I was. I told both of them that there had been an abuse complaint filed against me.

Amy Lynn erupted. "IF THEY SAY I SAID ANYTHING, THEY ARE LYING BECAUSE, BECAUSE I DID NOT!!!"

"You said something," Stephen said, dryly. "You're always saying something."

Amy Lynn went into hissy fit mode. "I DID NOT. WHY DO YOU ALWAYS…"

"Amy Lynn," I said. "It doesn't matter. I think they are only doing it because I made them mad and now they are trying to punish me. I just want you to know what's going on, in case you hear anything. They will probably be calling your teachers, so your teachers might ask you questions. Just answer truthfully."

162

We took Stephen to Martial Arts, then Amy and I went to Dunkin' Donut's for cocoa, as we often did. It was time to give her a little more information. It was time to let her know that she was leaving.

"You know, Amy," I said, "It was your social worker who filed the complaint after that time she came out to visit you. So this is about you, not Stephen."

"Ooooh, I hate her!" she said.

I took a deep breath. "I believe they are going to move you to another foster home."

She sat back hard in her seat, but was surprisingly calm. "Why?"

"They think I am hurting you."

"But you're not. I don't want to go."

"Lesley has spent a lot of time on the phone with them, trying to work something out, but they are pretty determined to go ahead with this."

She started to cry quietly.

I felt bad that I wasn't being completely honest. I knew at some point I had to tell her that her earlier stories had something to do with this too. That I had something to do with it. But this didn't seem to be the moment.

"Come over here," I said, and Amy came around the table and buried her face in my neck. We hugged for a few minutes, but she soon became concerned that her cocoa would get cold. She complained about the unfairness of it all, but she didn't go into any Amy Lynn histrionics.

"Amy, do you remember when you told me that every foster home you had been in was better than the one before?"

"Yeah."

"Maybe the next one will be the best one yet."

"Maybe they'll have a swimming pool."

"Maybe so."

For the rest of that week Amy Lynn vacillated between anger at Pat Gibson and hope for that swimming pool. She spent a lot of time on my lap. That Saturday, she went to visit her mother.

The phone rang halfway through the afternoon. It was her mother's number on Caller ID, so I was surprised when it was Pat Gibson voice on the other end of the phone.

"I'm out here with Amy Lynn and her mother. I told her that you wanted her removed and I need to know what my deadline is. What is the last possible day that you will keep her?" I could hear Amy Lynn crying in the background.

If I could have reached through the phone, it wouldn't have been Amy I'd be accused of hurting. I reacted with my usual calm facade.

"Wednesday. I believe Lesley already made that clear."

"Just double checking." she said.

Just making sure Amy Lynn knows it is me, I thought.

"I'll be out to get her myself Wednesday morning."

I was glad Amy at least had her mother there to comfort her when she got the bad news. But mostly I was just sick about the whole thing. I rehearsed speeches to explain myself to Amy Lynn as if she was the parent and I was the child.

I expected anger, maybe a tantrum, at the very least, rejection. But instead, when she got out of the car in the driveway Amy Lynn ran straight into my arms.

"She tried to tell me it was your idea and I said, 'You're lying to me. Mary would never do that! She loves me!' I hate Pat Gibson!" she said with a fierce pride.

I stood in the driveway and hugged her while she cried.

Later that evening I asked her to sit down at the kitchen table and talk to me. I explained how it had all come about, from the beginning. She listened closely and responded with more maturity than most adults would.

She said she wished she didn't have that "bad habit" of lying, that she was sorry for the trouble she caused. I said I was sorry too for the runaway train I had started and told her I wished she could stay. We hugged and hugged and then started packing.

When Amy Lynn was at home, I had to deal with her emotions first and foremost. When she was at school, I had to deal with the situation from a different angle, the legal one.

The first thing I did when I found out about the complaint against me was to call Stephen's DHS worker, Judith Taylor, and inform her. As I expected, she was sympathetic and supportive. She reassured me that complaints against foster parents almost always ended up called "un-substantiated," that it was an unwritten rule. She also said she would do some snooping behind the scenes and see if she could find out the content of the complaint.

Then I called Stephen's guardian *ad litem*, who made me feel better by reacting with shock and anger, but advised strongly that I get a lawyer. I went through the phone book with her on the phone and read off names. She gave me recommendations and I made some calls. I ended up with an appointment to meet with Barbara Raimondi within days.

Barbara was wonderful. She called DHS herself, stating that she was representing me in this matter and asking for a copy of the complaint. Interestingly, each and every person she talked to, Pat Gibson, her supervisor Michelle Gauthier, their supervisor, sounded shocked that I had retained a lawyer, said they would get back to her, and then never did. She followed up with a letter. There was no response.

On her advice, I called people whom I thought DHS might be calling so they would hear the news from me first. I called Amy's teachers, a former teacher she was still in contact with, her former foster mother and her Pediatrician. I was too late. The social worker who never had time to return my calls had found time to call all of them. The conversations, as related to me, went something like this:

"Did Amy Lynn ever complain to you about the way she was treated by Mary Callahan?"

"Oh, she complained when things didn't go her way. Then she raved about Mary the next day when things were better."

"What did she complain about specifically?"

"She'd say she was left locked in a closet, or that she was only fed bread and water. Amy Lynn had all kinds of stories about everyone."

"Why would you think these stories aren't true?"

"Because Amy Lynn was well dressed and well fed. Mary came to every school program and Amy Lynn would run up to her and hug her. She was the happiest I'd ever seen her, but she still had a temper on her bad days."

"Is there anything else you want to report? Anything else Amy Lynn told you about her home life?"

I kept in touch with Barbara by email and we kept each other informed of every conversation or unreturned phone call. Judith and Lesley called when they got new information.

I sent the following letter to DHS:

Michelle Gauthier, Supervisor
DHS Lewiston
Lewiston, Maine 04240

Dear Ms. Gauthier,

I understand you have expressed concerns about the quality of care given to foster children in my home, in particular Amy Lynn Jones. I would like to respond that I have serious concerns of my own about the service and support provided by your office on Amy Lynn's behalf.

I accepted Amy Lynn into my home after meeting her and after lengthy conversations with then worker Laurel Robertson. Laurel was warm, intelligent and responsive. Soon after taking Amy Lynn I learned that Laurel would be leaving and replaced by Pat Gibson. I was introduced to Pat Gibson at a Network meeting. Pat said nothing during the meeting, and barely made eye contact, let alone spoke to me when introduced afterwards. A few minutes later I was wandering the halls of DHS looking for the bathroom. I ran into Pat at the elevator and asked for directions. She did not answer or even look at me.

Communications have not improved since. I leave messages on Pat's voice mail and she does not call back. She leaves terse messages on my machine (always on the day I said I wouldn't be home) with her own issues, but does not offer any response to the issue I called her about in the first place. As you know I reached the end of my rope with this two months ago. The first week in December I left messages on Pat Edward's voice mail about problems with Amy's behavior. In addition to the behavior she had begun to tell stories at school and in the neighborhood that she was being mistreated in my home. Specifically, she told four different people that she was kept locked in the basement and not fed, that I called her a bitch and a heathen and that she was not getting any Christmas presents. I left this information for Pat and her response was to ignore it completely. Instead she left three different messages on my machine:

1. She did not believe I was telling the truth regarding one of Amy Lynn's weekend ride screw ups,
2. I would be responsible for driving Amy to see her mother from now on, and
3. We would be sticking with the same counselor for Amy in spite of my letter stating I would not take Amy Lynn to this person any more.

There was no mention of the message I left. Just an accusation of lying, orders to give up 4 hours every Saturday to driving and complete invalidation of my observations regarding Amy's counselor.

I have told everyone from Amy's teachers to her guardian *ad litem*, that the reason I gave notice on her is because a child who makes up stories and an unsupportive team is a recipe for disaster. And now, after I have been very patient in extending my time with her, you are making my prediction come true. This serves only to prove my point, not only about the recipe for disaster but also about the lack of support. I think "lack of support" is actually a little mild. I would describe Pat Gibson as hostile from the first time I met her.

Complaints about Pat Gibson do not end with my communications problems. Amy's Medicaid card has never been switched to my address. Paperwork that was supposed to be sent to Agency C was never sent. I have not been notified of Network meetings even though I have asked to be. Amy's teachers complain that they leave messages for Pat Gibson and get no response either.

The arrangements for Amy's visits with her mother have been disastrous. Once we were told to expect a driver at 9 A.M. and none came. Instead a ride we hadn't been told of came for her at 4 P.M. That evening I got a phone call from someone who said she had been sitting in my driveway at 9 A.M. waiting, but gave up on us. She had been given a wrong address. And thank goodness for that. As it turned out, Amy's mother had only been informed of the 4 P.M. ride and would not have been home if Amy had been delivered in the morning. As I was also going out for the day, there would have been no place for a driver to bring Amy back to either.

Pat Gibson never even met Amy Lynn until I called the guardian *ad litem* to complain about it. When she did visit, some time after I gave my 30 days notice, Pat spent time alone with Amy and then did not inform me of whether or not Amy had been told she was leaving. I received no phone call at all after the visit.

And as far as the counselor, Theresa Jo Johnson, I will reiterate what I said in my letter about her. I gave her three chances. I spoke to her about my concerns twice. Her defensive response only confirmed to me that she is a *bad* counselor. I would not take my biological children to her and I will do no less for a foster child. Amy is not attached to her. She had to be coaxed and begged to get in the car to go see her. I communicated all this with DHS every step of the way on the phone and in writing. In the end, you chose to demonstrate a complete lack of respect for my role. (I am your eyes and ears when it comes to Amy Lynn, am I not? You're not here.) And you chose to leave that information in yet another message on my answering machine.

Lastly, if you want to know what kind of care Amy is really getting, talk to someone who knows. I can give you a list of teachers, neighbors, respite workers and baby-sitters who have far more information on this household than Pat Gibson has. Ask them. Ask Amy. She is doing fine. She never was the problem.

Sincerely,

Mary Callahan

I never received a response.

CHAPTER 23

A Story About
Three Chickens

Amy Lynn left on Wednesday as planned. Pat Gibson sent a stranger to transport her. Amy gave me a mobile that she made as a going away present and I gave her a ring with a cubic zirconium and platinum filigree. She gave me a note as she left that said, "I am gwon to miss you, but well wolwise be together in love. P.S. Keep ore job you are the gret fostemom."

That evening I got a call from her new foster mom, Linda. It seems she had received a phone call just the day before asking her to consider taking Amy Lynn. She said she would think about it and the next morning a car pulled in her driveway with Amy Lynn and all her belongings. The driver had no information except "This child makes up stories, so be careful." She was only able to find me because Amy Lynn knew our phone number.

Linda and I agreed to keep in touch, and then Amy Lynn got on the phone. "You were right! They have a swimming pool."

Having an abuse complaint filed against me caused practical problems as well as anxiety. I was unable to take a second placement, but I didn't want one. My finances were back in enough order that I could work 24

hours a week at the hospital and pay the bills. The last thing I wanted was another placement. I thought I would never want or accept a child again.

The problem was that I couldn't change agencies, so my job was still a secret between Lesley and I. I wondered if the new agency would still want me when it was over. If they didn't, Agency B and Lesley would probably be forced to keep me, and the job would become an issue.

Of course there was always the possibility the complaint would be deemed substantiated and I would lose my foster care license and Stephen. That was, of course, my greatest fear. Judith had heard from the Lewiston office of DHS questioning why she had let Stephen stay with me so long when I was so "unfit." She defended me ferociously, but was shaken by the call. Lesley had been accused of letting the abuse go on, but still didn't know what abuse. We all knew we could be waiting a very long time for answers.

As it turned out, it was only two weeks after Amy Lynn left when I finally had the complaint read to me on the phone. Judith had seen it before that, but had to get permission to share it with me. When she did, I laughed out loud. It was so ridiculous. It was not about locking the child up or starving her. It was just the most minimal of Amy Lynn's complaints. Reading between the lines, I think poor Amy was really holding back when she had the opportunity to tell one of her fantastic stories and instead just did some minor whining. There were three specific complaints:

1. Amy Lynn thought I liked Stephen more than her,
2. She didn't like worrying about whether or not she would get Barbie dolls for Christmas.
3. I told a story about three chickens that she didn't like.

I have no idea what story she is referring to. None of the kids remember a story that involves chickens. The closest we could come was a story about turkeys and how stupid they are. My daughter Renee didn't like that story because it involved turkeys ending up covered in turkey poop and Renee thought it was undignified of me to be telling stories that gross. But Amy Lynn had a way of adopting other people's stories as her own, so that may have been it. Or maybe some other mother did tell a story about three chickens that she didn't like. Who knows. But in any case I was relieved that I wasn't being accused of anything more substantial.

Judith said she would have been embarrassed to put her name on that complaint. She also let me know that Pat Gibson was leaving DHS, and "it wasn't entirely voluntary." I hoped it had something to do with my letter. I would never know, as her supervisor never responded to it.

Within a week I was informed that the complaint was kicked from "abuse investigation" to potential "licensing violation." That was an improvement. I was able to discharge my lawyer, pay her $375 bill and fight it myself, but I still couldn't change agencies and I still had to be dishonest with Lesley.

Finally, I got a call from my licensing worker, Wendy, and we made an appointment for her to come out to do her investigation. I had met Wendy one other time, when I first moved to Lisbon. She was very pleasant. She seemed sensible and logical, something that was hard to come by in a social worker, but she also seemed young and inexperienced. I could tell she wanted to do her job well, but it didn't come naturally yet. She came out with another woman whom she referred to as a "student." I wondered if she brought her along as a witness because she had heard I was a tough one.

We talked at my kitchen table for about an hour. It seemed to go well. The tone was friendly and I did not end up feeling as if I were under attack. As she left she told me that it all seemed like a tempest in a teapot and she would run it by her supervisors, but she felt it would amount to nothing.

I was relieved, but I did not believe it would amount to "nothing." Once Wendy was back in her office, the powers above her would help her find one thing to say I had done wrong to justify the complaint being filed in the first place. And that is exactly what happened.

Wendy called a few weeks later. I could almost hear in her voice that she was speaking someone else's words. She said the complaint was going to be labeled unsubstantiated, but, "There is some concern about the way you handled the reading issue with Amy Lynn. Telling her that she might not get what she wants for Christmas unless she learns to read could be considered emotional abuse. Christmas should never be used as a bargaining tool."

I only argued a little. Later I thought I might have mentioned the line "He knows if you've been bad or good, so be good for goodness sake," in the famous Christmas song and asked if that was emotionally abusive. I held my tongue partly because I was glad it was over and partly because I didn't think Wendy was the one to blame anyway.

The complaint was dropped. Amy Lynn was gone. And I swore I would never take another foster child. I made people promise to throw themselves on the ground in front of me if I ever started moving towards getting another foster child. It would be Stephen and me from now on, with our wonderful team of Judith and Carolee and whoever took Lesley's place.

I called Linda and Amy Lynn once a week for a while. I asked if we could drive up for a visit and Linda admitted she was disobeying a DHS warning just by letting Amy Lynn talk to me on the phone, so it was a bad idea to visit. Eventually, she stopped returning my calls, so I took that as my signal the Amy was doing well and stopped calling.

The happiest pictures on the mantel are of Amy Lynn. There is one of her in a Cleopatra wig, another of her getting a piggy back ride on Tony's back, another of her sticking her tongue out at me through a window. She was quite a character.

Stephen

One of the nursing supervisors came to me after my first editorial was in the Sunday paper. She has known me for some time and knew I has foster kids, so I was surprised to be getting new information from her.

"I had two nieces in foster care," she told me. "My sister had a drug problem and deserted them."

"What happened?" I asked, noting that she spoke in the past tense. "Are they back home?"

"They have been adopted by strangers," she told me. "My parents tried to get custody. We all tried. But DHS believes the apple doesn't fall far from the tree. They wouldn't believe we aren't all like my sister." She had tears in her eyes. "We know they'll be back when they turn eighteen. They knew they were loved."

CHAPTER 24

✦ ✦ ✦

"It Wasn't My Mom's Fault"

Stephen was my first treatment level child. He has been with me for three years, through Marie's leaving as well as the comings and goings of Tina, Brian and Amy Lynn. I have been with him through good times and bad. We have a connection. We both hope that he stays with me until he ages out of the system. Only I realize that is not guaranteed.

The reason Stephen's placement has lasted is not him or me. It is his team. Judith, his DHS worker, and Carolee, his guardian *ad litem* have also been with me through thick and thin. Both were new to his case when I got him. We all got to know him together. And through it all they seemed to remember two things more than anyone else I have dealt with in this business:

Everyone deserves to be treated with respect.
The child's needs come first.

They treat me with the utmost respect, always returning phone calls, sympathizing with me when sympathy was what I need and offering real tangible help, like transportation or childcare when I can't provide it.

Judith reminds me of a teacher my autistic son Tony had when he was at his most difficult. At least once a week that teacher told me what a great job I was doing. It energized me. Sometimes it was all I needed to survive. With Judith I end up laughing every time I have to call about some outrageous thing Stephen has done. Like the time he smeared feces on his bedroom wall (he only did it once) and the biting stage he went through (he truly believed he was a vampire). She always says, "I am so sorry," as if *she* did something wrong! I have to reassure her that I'll get through it, but I am happy to get through it with her acknowledgment that it is difficult, instead of some reminder that I am well paid or that it is in my contract.

Carolee is devoted to Stephen's entire family. She takes the siblings to see each other on her free time. She inspires me to do the same and to understand why those connections are so necessary to maintain. The day will come when Stephen wakes up and realizes that everyone who loves him is paid to love him. That is unless I keep his biological family in the picture. They are the ones who have to fight to love him.

Stephen was treatment level when I got him. By definition that means that he is especially difficult, five times as difficult as Marie based on the pay increase. Of course, Marie was a teenager when Steve moved in and what could be more difficult than that?

The primary reason I changed to treatment level was so I could afford to quit my job and be home to keep her out of trouble. So his addition to the family served a financial purpose, as well as a practical one.

Unfortunately, it was six weeks after I quit my job before I finally got a treatment level child so I had to work every per diem shift I could get at any hospital in the meantime. The plan to supervise Marie more was preceded by six weeks of supervising her less while I worked primarily night shifts and bugged the foster care agency for a referral.

My agency worker's name was Evelyn. We talked on the phone regularly, but there was never any news. There were no treatment level kids waiting for a home.

When I worked nights, I left a message on her machine, instructing her not to call before 2 P.M. the next day, so I could have uninterrupted sleep. She always called at 11 A.M.

"Good morning Mary. I just wanted you to know we have no referrals today, but I've heard there might be one tomorrow."

Stunned out of a deep sleep, I was barely able to comprehend what was being said, but I knew enough not to sound miffed.

"Okay." I mumbled, "What do you know about the one that might be coming in?"

"Not much. The worker left a message on my machine that she would call me before the day is over. If it sounds appropriate for you, I'll call you tomorrow."

"Okay."

"Are you working tonight?"

"Yes."

"So I should call after two, like today, right?"

"Yes." Now I was confused. "Is my clock wrong? I've got eleven o'clock."

"No, it is eleven o'clock."

"Okay. So you'll call me tomorrow after two if there is a child for me to look at?" I asked, finally clearing some of the fog.

"Right."

The next morning at eleven she called to say the referral would not be appropriate for me.

I kept wondering how she could be so dense, but then, quite by accident, I met her at an educational seminar and decided she wasn't being dense, but passive/aggressive.

The seminar was huge, held in a big auditorium, and filled to capacity. I didn't think I knew anyone there until I turned to the pretty blond woman sitting next to me and read her name tag.

"Evelyn," I said, surprised. "Evelyn from Agency B?"

"Yes," she said, looking at my name tag.

"I'm Mary Callahan! Isn't that funny. We talk on the phone almost every day."

She smiled a weak smile and agreed it was quite a coincidence, but quickly turned to the person on the other side of her and began to whisper. She didn't turn back to me after the program began. When I returned from the first coffee break, she and her friend had found new seats.

I have to remind myself sometimes that these people, these professionals who seem to exist only to annoy me, probably went into this field with the best of intentions. They probably had hero fantasies just like mine. Before they gave into their power and control fantasies. I wonder what it is that changes them. Evelyn finally left Agency B and I got Stephen from her replacement, Rusty.

That was a relief. Rusty was like Laurel, Amy Lynn's first worker, funny, down to earth, and intelligent. We clicked immediately. I was optimistic after he told me all about Stephen, that I would not only enjoy the child but I would enjoy working with Rusty with regard to him. Unfortunately, Rusty was fired shortly after I got Stephen. Not a team player, I was told.

But the day I drove down to Sanford to meet Stephen, all was right with the world. As I drove, I mulled over the conversation I'd had with the group home leader when I made these arrangements.

"Stevie, Stevie, Stevie." he said. "Our little Stevie is finally leaving."

"Why do you say that?" I asked. "Is he hard to place?"

"No, he's hard to give up. He was only supposed to be here a month and we've kept him for three."

"Why is he leaving now? Did DHS catch up with you?"

"No. He's starting to show his true colors, so we made the call."

"True colors?"

"Oh, just typical kid stuff," he backpedaled. "Fighting with other kids and all. He's a little bit manipulative. They all are."

Yes, but they don't all stay two months over their deadline, I thought. He must really be a charmer. But only with adults who have control over him. It is typical behavior for kids who have been bounced around a lot. They learn to read adults and figure out how to win them over. But they don't waste any of that skill on relationships with other children. Why bother? Other children have no power.

I was surprised when I met Steve to see that he was significantly overweight. That usually doesn't endear adults, though it might be part of the reason he had trouble getting along with other kids. Again, I realized he must really be able to pour on the charm, for adults to overlook his size.

As we walked around the neighborhood together, on our get acquainted visit, I saw it for myself. This kid was good. But I was careful not to fall under his spell. I did my best to just listen and learn and prepare.

The first thing I learned was that he was not only big, but out of shape. He complained that his feet hurt and had to sit for breaks frequently, but I knew it wasn't his feet. He was flushed, sweaty and panting by the time we sat.

Because of that, I had mixed feeling when I saw a Dairy Queen up ahead. With any other child, it would have been the perfect place to continue our conversation. With Stephen it felt like giving a cigarette to an asthmatic.

I compromised by suggesting an ice cream cone, mentally stepping back from the bigger treats on the menu. He wasn't happy.

"I want a hot fudge sundae."

"I didn't offer that." I said. "I offered an ice cream cone."

"Then I want it dipped in chocolate with sprinkles."

"I didn't offer that either. The only question is whether you want chocolate or vanilla."

"That is so not fair!"

"Then I guess the only question is whether you want an ice cream cone or not. We could just keep walking."

"No, no. I want the ice cream cone. Chocolate. Large."

"Medium."

It was his only moment of being less than charming. The rest of the time he was delightful. He asked questions about me, about Marie, about our house. He laughed at my jokes. It was more like talking with another adult, even an adult male who was courting a bit, than talking with a child.

Eventually, he told me about himself, giving a quick summary of his life and how it had led him to be in the position of needing a new home. He explained that his mother was too young when she started to have babies.

"She was 14 when my brother was born, then two years later she had me, then my sister two years after that. She didn't know how to raise kids. She always called one of her brothers when she didn't know what to do and they would come over and spank us. Then one time my Uncle Shane snapped a towel at me after his shower and it hit me over my eye. I was supposed to tell the teacher that my brother did it, but I forgot. So the next day, DHS came and took us. They put my brother with Grammy and my sister with her real father, but I went to live with Chrissy."

As I would learn was typical of Stephen, he didn't have a bad word to say about anyone. He loved his first foster mother Chrissy, and he

179

had nothing but understanding when she called DHS to come get him because she was getting a divorce.

"She couldn't handle me by herself," he told me; though to hear him talk she was already doing it by herself. Stephen could barely remember her husband, except his name, Jon.

Stephen was thrilled when he was placed next with Aunt Holly and Uncle Joe, because their boy Joseph was his favorite cousin. But he explained that it was hard for them and that he and Joseph "did some bad things," so he had to leave their home too. He was then sent to the diagnostic center called Pace where I met him (though, to this day, Stephen calls it Paste). He said it was a blast.

When I commented that his life had been hard, Stephen was quick to tell me it wasn't his mother's fault. I didn't think I had implied it was. He wanted me to know right up front, even if he was going to move in with me, she was his real boss, as in "You're not the boss of me." After all, he told me, she gave him life and no one else can do that.

I knew a lot about Stephen by the time I drove back to Portland that day. I knew we would have the weight issue to deal with, the manipulative behavior, and the inability to get along with kids his own age. I knew better than he did that those "bad things" he did with his cousin would be a factor in his life for a very long time. And I knew his loyalty would always be to his real family.

I also knew I wanted him. I wanted to give him security, a soft place to fall.

CHAPTER 25

✦ ✦ ✦

Depressing the Counselor

Stephen moved in, started school, and began to antagonize Marie all in short order. The first surprise was when he told his class, by way of introducing himself, that he had watched dirty movies. His teacher changed the subject and I had a talk with him about it afterwards. He told me that he and his cousin had watched a lot of movies "with naked ladies" and I wondered why anyone was surprised when they went on to act out some of the scenes from those movies.

I gather Uncle Joe nearly flipped when he walked in on the two boys and immediately had Stephen removed. PACE was supposed to evaluate his level of dysfunction. They determined that the behavior was mutual and not surprising for two boys left alone in their room for long periods of time after watching pornography. In spite of their report, Stephen would be in counseling as a perpetrator of sexual abuse for years.

For me that meant two things, keeping a close eye on him around younger kids and driving him to counseling. It should have meant more.

✦ ✦ ✦

I read magazines in the waiting room while Stephen was in with his counselor. Every now and then I gave the man a bit of information from Stephen's week, but mostly I considered that hour a nice break for me.

Sometimes Stephen had homework from counseling. Once he was told to look at himself in the mirror before going to bed and tell himself that what he did with Joseph was wrong and that he would never do it again. It seemed like shaming to me, something I sought to avoid with kids, but I deferred to the expert.

Then one day, about a year after Stephen moved in, the counselor asked me to join them for a session. The first thing on his mind was Brian.

Brian had moved in about four days before. He was sitting in the waiting room with me when the counselor came out for Stephen. He wanted to know who he was and I explained.

"He needs to know about Stephen's history," he told me.

I was stunned. "Well, maybe in time," I stammered. "Right now he has enough of his own problems."

"No, now," he said. "There can be no secrets between family members."

Stephen sat there and fidgeted while we argued.

"I believe that violates confidentiality," I said.

"Safety is more important than confidentiality."

"Brian is safe. I am always watching them. Besides, he's four years older than Stephen. He'd pop him one if he tried anything."

It was a tough sell, but I was finally able to convince him that I would decide when the time was right to tell Brian of Stephen's history of sex play with a younger cousin.

If the time is ever right, I thought to myself. For the first time I was looking at this man and wondering why I had ever left Stephen alone with him. He did have a fairly odd affect, kind of dark and brooding, for a person who works with children. Stephen never expressed any affection for him, just dread of counseling.

As I sat in that chair I realized that I would never have taken one of my biological children to him. Nor would I have sat in the waiting room and assumed the right things were going on behind closed doors. Because Stephen was a foster child, I let someone else make the decisions. I abdicated my responsibility to *think*.

A year had gone by without me realizing Stephen's counselor was a nut. But I was off the hook in a matter of minutes.

There was a second reason he had called me back to the office that day.

"I have decided to quit my practice," he told us. "I have become so depressed listening to children's stories that I have found my only joy in life is retelling their stories to my friends as if they are jokes. I've come to realize that is inappropriate and I need to get out of this line of work."

My eyes must have popped out of my head. "Okay, then," I said, taking the little widget Stephen was fooling with out of his hands, "then we'll be going now."

I took Stephen's hand and headed out the door. Thank goodness the hallway was long and I had time to shake my head a few times and change my expression back to normal by the time we got to Brian.

Judith was horrified when I told her what went on that day. We both agreed that Stephen probably needed counseling to recover from the counselor as much as anything, but that a break from counseling was probably the next best thing.

While he did go back into counseling later to try to deal with other issues, like fighting at school, the sexual issues were dropped. The second counselor was unsuccessful at getting Stephen to engage because he was so bitter about being back in counseling at all. After about six months, Judith and I decided to stop it for good.

This was not a simple decision. To qualify as a treatment level child, Stephen is supposed to be in counseling. The choices were to keep in counseling for that reason, drop him to family level and lose $2000 a month, or start a different form of therapy which involved a person who comes into our home called a Family Integration Specialist.

That person needs only a high school education and some on the job training. We chose the Family Integration Specialist. The first one quit without notice after the second visit. The second one takes Stephen out with a group of boys like himself, in foster care. That has turned out to be fun and maybe even good for him.

Stephen has been with me for three years now without perpetrating against another child. He and I have had many a long talk about what happened between him and his cousin. He is haunted by it, but probably was much by its aftermath as the event itself. I still believe any two children left alone in a bedroom for hours after watching a pornographic movie would have done the same thing.

CHAPTER 26

✦ ✦ . ✦

Price Tags and Broccoli

I was on a mission from the minute Stephen moved in and that was to improve his health. Okay, that is a euphemism. I wanted him to lose weight. As it was, he couldn't even snap his jeans without me holding his belly up and out of the way. He, of course, didn't see a problem. He thought he would spend his time sitting in front of the TV eating junk food and I would drive him everywhere so his feet wouldn't hurt.

I didn't come right out and tell him his weight was an issue. But I told him that kids should be active and that I wanted to take walks and ride bikes until his feet got used to it. I never let his complaining stop me, but he never stopped complaining either.

Finally I hit on a controversial solution. I bought a trampoline. As an ER nurse, I know there are injuries every year from jumping on trampolines. But I decided that his health was at least as threatened by his inactivity. I would supervise well and take my chances.

I also enrolled him in Martial Arts training. He kicked and screamed over that, claiming it was stupid and boring, until after his first introductory session.

He walked out of there wanting to come back every day of his life to do it again. I have found martial arts to be good exercise as well as a great character builder. There is so much talk of respect for others and respect for oneself. Self-esteem grows each time one of the teachers gives a compliment, which is often.

Now, three years later, Stephen jumps on the trampoline almost every day and goes to Martial Arts twice a week. He is very good at Martial Arts, actually one of the more agile kids in the class. He took ski lessons this past winter and was quite good at that, too. His height and weight have barely changed, but a lot of the fat has turned to muscle. He is very active and much happier with himself.

The food issue has been harder to solve. With a history of being malnourished early in life, he had developed a real obsession with food. He talked about what he had eaten last and fretted about what he would eat next. He loved to list everything he had eaten in the past weeks. He loved to shop for food and prepare food.

I thought I had at last found a child who would appreciate my cooking, but I was wrong. He was a big eater, but a very picky one. Once I told him he could list five items that he didn't like and I would agree not to serve them. His items were fruits, vegetables, liver, seafood and any bread but white bread. When I said they had to be items, not groups of items, he couldn't come up with a list as short as five. So we settled on the tried and true, "Eat what I serve or you don't get dessert." Then I made sure we always had a good dessert. Now he eats pretty much everything but seafood and liver.

It seemed odd to me that a picky eater like Stephen had the strange habit of eating non-food items. Pica, the clinical term for eating of non-food items, was listed as an issue in the records, but one that was already solved. That turned out to be inaccurate.

Once we were sitting in an auditorium waiting for Marie's school talent show to begin and Stephen propped one foot up on the opposite knee and began to pick the crud from between the treads on the bottom of his sneakers. When he put it in his mouth, I screamed.

Another time, Tina screamed when he started eating the price tags off the clothes I had just bought for him. He thought it was funny that he could get such a reaction from us.

Now I believe he is old enough to be embarrassed by such behavior instead of amused. Plus, he has heard me say, "Anyone who eats price tags can eat broccoli" enough times to stop eating price tags.

I say I "believe" it has stopped, because I can't really be sure what he is doing when I don't have my eyes on him. I would have sworn he was not ingesting anything with lead in it, but when I had his lead level drawn about a year after he moved in, it was very high.

I learned quite inadvertently that Stephen had been treated with chelation therapy for lead poisoning when he lived in his first foster home. We were visiting someone in the hospital and when we walked by the flower shop, Stephen said, "I used to get a flower there every time I got my shot."

"What shot?"

"My lead shot."

"You got a lead shot?"

"Yeah. All the time."

Judith went through his massive hand written records and discovered what he was talking about. He had been found to have a dangerously high lead level in his first foster home. He had IV medication to bring it down as well as follow-up blood draws to check his progress.

It is amazing how a piece of information like that can get lost with foster kids. They move from place to place. Their files get so fat that only the recent information is brought to team meetings. Old problems are forgotten when new ones appear, even if the old ones needed monitoring.

I have never yet had a foster child whose immunization record made any sense. They change doctors every time they change foster homes. It takes months to get anything that resembles an immunization record and it typically has a check mark instead of a date next to each shot. I have taken kids for Hepatitis B shots only to learn after the fact that it was already done years before. I have faked immunization records to get kids into summer camp.

But Stephen's lead level took me down a path I am not sure was the right one. I am glad I learned of it for one reason. It gave me another excuse for keeping him on a healthy diet. Lead takes up the receptor sites meant for iron and calcium. Therefore the body has no place to store those two minerals. They move right on through, so it is important to have them in the diet every day and in large amounts. That's the way it was explained to me, and that is the way I explained it to Stephen to get him to buy into the healthy diet idea a little bit more. It worked. Now he not only memorizes what we have to eat every meal, but it's mineral content as well. Maybe he'll grow up to be a dietitian or a great chef.

But the path I regret taking was the one that led me to another behavior specialist.

Stephen's behavior and his schoolwork had a roller coaster quality to it. He could go along for months being a star student and then suddenly become the class clown or the class bully. He would be so proud of his schoolwork and then out of the blue, decide to blow it off. His behavior at home usually mirrored what was going on at school. If he was mouthing off to his teacher, he was mouthing off to me.

It crossed my mind that some of Stephen's behavior issues might be related to his lead level. Maybe, when his behavior deteriorated, it was because he had found a source of lead and his levels were up. I asked Judith if I could have a neuropsychiatric exam done to see if this was the case. She agreed and sent me to Dr. Julie Domino.

Dr. Domino spent two long mornings with Stephen. He wasn't thrilled to be there, but he cooperated, and typical of Stephen, he did his best to charm. The end result was that his behavior did not resemble that of lead-effected children, and therefore was unlikely to be related to that. His behavior did resemble that of a severely attachment disordered child.

The fact that Stephen had attachment issues was not a surprise. The fact that any child who has been bounced from place to place has attachment issues is not a surprise. I hesitate to even call it a disorder, because it is such a natural result of their lives. I see it as adaptive. They have learned a lesson in life and that is not to get attached to someone they will likely lose. I was developing attachment issues myself having so many kids come and go over the years.

But there were two things about Stephen that made his issues worth more than the usual amount of attention.

One, he manifested his attachment issues, not by being aloof and indifferent to his caretakers, as the label seems to imply, but by being overly and indiscriminately attached.

In other words, Stephen loved everyone. He hugged, petted and complimented everyone he came in contact with, with the exception of grown men, who he avoided or cowered around. He hugged me and told me he loved me so much I had to put limits on it. He hugged my friends, even friends he had never met before.

And periodically he asked when he would be moving on.

He loved me to death, but got bored with me and wanted to love some other foster parent to death. His attachment was fake. But also adaptive. People you love are more likely to love you back. And more likely to buy you stuff.

The other thing that came out of this evaluation was Dr. Domino's conviction that Stephen's problems were so severe that he would never attach to anyone unless his biological mother was cut out of the picture. She was actually concerned that he might be having episodes of dissociation, times when he emotionally left the scene to protect himself from the pain.

I was shocked at her report. I knew dissociation was part of multiple personality disorder. I had asked for the evaluation because of the sudden deterioration in his behavior I witnessed the winter after he moved in. I thought it might be related to lead ingestion, but I never considered that he might be another personality when he was acting out.

I felt bad because I knew she got that, not from testing Stephen, but from things I told her. I had told her that he argued with himself in his sleep in two different voices. It spooked me when I heard it but I didn't think of it as THAT serious.

I had also told her of the time he was allowed to go to a family reunion for the weekend with his aunt and uncle and came back withdrawn and non-communicative. He barely spoke at all for two days. He fell asleep with his head in a bowl of cereal one morning and messed his pants on the school bus with no embarrassment whatsoever.

She felt he was dissociating at that time. I had taken him to the doctor on the third day and he had bilateral ear infections, but she said that wouldn't have caused the behavior.

I was shocked to think that his problems were so severe, but also shocked at the solution. I had taken great pains to keep him in touch with his family. I was proud of that. Now it seemed like I might have missed the mark again, just like when I kept taking him to the bad counselor.

We had a team meeting. Dr. Domino came and presented her results. Judith got to be the one to tell Stephen that he wouldn't be seeing his mother anymore. I got to enforce it.

Whether cutting him off from his mother was a mistake or not sticking with that now is a mistake, we may never know. How does one know for sure? If he turns out badly, who is to say that he might not have turned out worse, were it not for something I did or didn't do?

I guess it is no different than with biological kids. You try to make the right decisions. Sometimes you question the decisions you make. But there is never a moment you can point to and say, "That's when I made the critical mistake," or "That's when I saved the day." Because, of course, you never know what would have happened if you made the opposite decision.

But, in any case, we couldn't stick with our conviction that Stephen needed a parentectomy. We lasted a little over a year.

Part of the reason we failed was probably the fact that we did maintain his connection with all his other family members. We visited his brother in his group home. We had his half-sister and his cousin over for visits. And all they ever talked about was Mom.

They talked about the "good old days" with Mom. They told Stephen about their last contact with her. He gave them messages to give her. It seemed ridiculous to me. It was like Mom was a carrot on a stick we were dangling just out of his reach, even when he did have visits with her. After those stopped, it was like we were just dangling the carrot a little farther away. She was still a factor in his life. And he still had every intention of going back to her when he was eighteen.

Every time the team got together we talked about it. None of us was terribly comfortable with it. We talked about reversing the decision. I hesitated because I thought, after we told him it was definite and permanent, we needed to stand by that. After all, we blamed Mom for her inconsistency, canceling visits at the last minute and such. How could we then be just as inconsistent?

But one day I went to a lecture and heard the speaker say something that changed my mind. He said that the $100,000 kids, of whom Stephen was one based on the fact that he was treatment level, had a 0% chance of leading productive lives as adults. He said, "To a child, if you check up on them at age 25, they will be in a correctional facility or a mental health institution."

I was stunned again. Most people quickly argue that the kids with the most problems in the first place are the treatment level kids so, of course, they have the worst prognosis.

But I wondered if we had the cause and effect in reverse. I knew Stephen. I'm not going to say he didn't have problems, but I would not have predicted either outcome for him. And anyway, the things that brought out his anger (which could lead to criminal behavior) or made him sad (which could lead to mental health problems) were not the events of his past, but the things the system was doing to him in the present.

And even if I was wrong about that, I argued at the next team meeting, if he really has no future, why not give him what he wants now? What he wants is time with his mother.

We talked about it, agreed to think about it. Judith had to run it by her supervisor. We had just about come to a consensus to throw out Dr. Domino's recommendations when something else unexpected happened.

Terrorists flew airplanes into buildings one Tuesday morning.

I didn't even know about it when Judith showed up at my door for the team meeting. I thought she was crazy when she said, "I don't know if we should bother with this meeting. We're being bombed, you know. They have already hit New York and Washington."

I kept repeating, "What are you talking about?" until she made me turn on the TV.

Once we got the general idea, and in my mind that was the fact that we might all be dead soon, we looked at each other and said, "Stephen needs to call his mother."

Judith picked him up from school and brought him home to make the call. I think that was the moment that we all accepted the fact that she was his mother and always would be. His attachment is to her and any lack of attachment elsewhere is okay with us.

Now, seven months later, Stephen spends one afternoon a week with his mother, her new husband, and their thriving two year old. This summer it will be one full day a week. Stephen loves it, but he comes back worried about her financial situation.

"My mom never goes to movies," he tells me. "She can't afford it." I go to the movies during his visit.

"My mom only has two pair of shoes. How many do you have, like a hundred?"

I don't have a hundred, but the number is closer to that than it is to two.

"You don't even work full time and my mom works every day."

He knows I get paid to have him, but he doesn't know how much. If he did, which he will some day, he will see that something is dreadfully wrong with this system. He might even hate me for being a part of it. They pay me $2500 a month to raise somebody else's child, while that somebody else struggles for every dime. She is actually supposed to be paying the state a portion of her income as child support for Stephen. I hope she isn't. All this because she was raped at 13, then found solace in a man two more times before she was 18, then found solace in the bottle.

Reunification is not an option, because she didn't get her act together, stop drinking and settle down, in the eighteen months the state gave her to do it. I reap the benefits.

As do two social workers, one family integration specialist, their supervisors, the occasional therapist, and one lawyer. All of our incomes depend on kids like Stephen staying in the system and staying at the highest level of care, Treatment Level.

CHAPTER 27

✦ ✦ ✦

Biting the Hand That Feeds

I find myself wishing Stephen's story was more interesting. Of course, that is for the sake of the book. For him and for myself, I'm glad it's a little dull.

Not that we haven't had behavior problems. He did smear feces on his bedroom walls once and that will justify keeping him at treatment level for the rest of his stay in foster care. He was angry because I had put an alarm on his bedroom door after the incident with Tina under his covers. Unfortunately, he has this strange habit of having his bowel movement at 6 o'clock every morning and that meant waking the rest of the house up by setting the alarm off or holding it for an hour longer. There was a third option, but one I hadn't considered. Guess he showed me!!!

Obviously he must have been very, very angry to do something like that. And typical of Steve, it didn't show in his face. He looked up at me with wide eyes and said the dog did it. But then he couldn't explain how a pair of his socks got covered with it and were in the clothes hamper in his room. He finally admitted that he had put them on his hands to do the wall painting.

He had to clean every bit of the mess and got some kind of restrictions for punishment. He never did it again, but I soon took the alarm off the door, too.

Then there was his biting phase. He bit Brian. He bit me. He bit a girl in his class he particularly liked. He couldn't explain why at first, but then confided in me that he truly believed he was a vampire. He was a vampire every year for Halloween. He loved to wear his vampire costume around the house. And his nightmares all had vampires in them. When he wrote a paper about vampires for school, his teacher made an interesting observation.

"Once a vampire bites you, then you become a vampire too, right?" I agreed.

"So the one doing the biting just got himself a new family member and one that cannot go back, one that won't ever leave you, right?"

"Right."

"And Stephen only bites people he likes."

I talked to Stephen about that when I got home. He laughed. Then he started announcing before he bit that you would soon be part of his family.

But he didn't bite as hard and he soon stopped biting altogether. Now he tells people about the time he bit a girl in his class because he thought if he did she would have to like him because she would be a vampire with him. It is one of those funny family stories and he tells it on himself. He was a wizard for Halloween this past year.

I love a quick fix. Especially when there are no battles over it with team members. We brainstorm. I try something out. They might talk to him about whatever it is. Most problems resolve themselves in time.

He is a challenge, but no more than my own kids, Tony and Renee, were.

My biggest frustration now is with the private agency I joined when I left Agency B. I'm becoming and expert on these agencies now that I am with my third. I have to say, I haven't found one I'm comfortable with yet.

I left Agency A because Marie was so bitter about living in an abusive foster home for so long. I left Agency B because of their policy against work outside the home. If I left Agency C, it would be because of the busywork.

With other agencies I met with the worker once a month and so did any child I had through them. They wrote up reports. I documented BIG incidents and medical appointments. With Agency A, I turned in a one page monthly report.

With Agency C, I am to document on each child daily. I meet with the worker every two weeks and we choose four goals for each child and those are what I am to write about. I write every incident or conversation around those four goal as well as how much time I spent on each goal.

I dislike spending time writing about the kids that I could be spending with the kids, but I particularly dislike involving them in it. Agency C has a policy that kids need to be involved in picking their four goals and discussing their own progress.

I am reminded of Marie's protest, "I am not a science experiment!"

It is like having to make four New Years resolutions and being monitored on your progress every two weeks. I can't imagine that does much for self-esteem.

I try to diffuse it as much as I can by letting them know that I think it is ridiculous. When they don't want to talk about some issue at a team meeting, I give them a few lines to say that should satisfy the worker, whether they have any relation to the truth or not.

I also have to attend many more mandatory trainings with Agency C. They put on their own instead of letting foster parents choose and go to the trainings that might be relevant to their particular child. I drive to Augusta and sit through an hour on psychotropic drugs when I don't have any children taking them.

The irony of that particular required lecture was that it was not really about psychotropic drugs anyway. None were even mentioned. It was just an hour on DHS requirements regarding medications. Though I had never heard it in five years as a foster parent and with two other agencies, I learned that medications are to be kept in a safe. And they can't all be kept in the same safe. They have to be separated into three safes, one for prescription drugs, and one for over-the-counter pills and a third for topicals like Neosporin or Visine. The one for prescription drugs has to be a double safe, a safe within a safe. And if the child needs a dose at a time when he was not at home, the safe had to go with the child, not an individual pill in an envelope. Someone in the audience asked, what happens if you are going to the beach? Do you have to take the safe to the beach? The answer was yes.

I've questioned many times how the rules could be so different for each contract agency and I am told the rules are not different. They are exactly the same. It is the interpretation of the rules that varies from agency to agency. I ask my DHS worker what the rules really are and she says the individual agencies make the rules.

All I know is that one definition of tyranny is having so many rules that no one can possibly follow them all. Everyone becomes a rule breaker, so everyone has something to fear. If one is not a "team player," the rules they are breaking will be found out and used as justification for any and all punishment.

If, somewhere down the line, DHS decides to retaliate against me and take my kids, they need only to look for those three safes. They won't find them.

But, in the meantime, I keep going to mandatory trainings and meetings and making notes about my kids' every word or mood change.

I put up with it all because I got a raise of $25 a day when I switched to Agency C. The part about being able to work turned out to be minor compared to that. The truth is, they don't "support" working outside the home at Agency C, they require it. When I tried to cut back, I was told that wasn't allowed. I did it anyway. I just didn't tell them.

It also turned out they don't really pay the baby-sitter, or help find a baby-sitter as they said they did when they were courting me. The day after I signed with them, they told me they "mis-spoke" with regard to that.

So, for the money, I write and talk about the kids when I ought to be raising them. I lie when I don't feel like telling the truth. I pretend to like people I don't like. I go to educational seminars that are worthless. I play the game. They are finally paying me enough to play the game. It's like they say, everyone has a price. For a mere $85 a day, I sold my soul to the system.

Would I have played the game better with Marie, Tina, Brian and Amy Lynn if they were paying me $85 a day? I guess we'll never know.

Now, you might notice that I have been referring to the kids instead of the kid, when I swore Stephen would be my one and only. The truth is, I caved in. Judith called and asked if I really meant it when I said I would never take another foster child. I said there could be only one exception and that was if the second child had the same team as Stephen.

Who knew the child she was talking about did come with the same team!

Annie moved in at the beginning of the school year. She was twelve at the time. I didn't ask a lot of questions about her past. I know her parents were never married and both reported the other to DHS for child abuse. They each have separate supervised visits now.

She has her issues. What foster child doesn't? But she was made a treatment level child for one reason and that because that is what I am licensed for and there were no other spots.

She lived with an aunt before me who was paid the standard kinship stipend of $137 a month. The behavior problems got to be too much for her. I get the standard treatment Foster parent stipend of $2500 a month. She'd have to have some pretty significant behavior problems for me to give that up.

Besides the $5000 per month I get for these two delightful kids, there is a separate budget that pays for clothes, recreation and summer camp. My credit card bills are evaporating. The kids go to respite for the weekend every three weeks, just so I won't get burned out. I have a great team to work with, plenty of money, a regularly scheduled break from parenting.

I have finally learned how to be a foster parent. Don't think too hard.

If DHS is a system that chews kids up and spits them out, I have cheerfully become a back molar…with a gold filling.

There are lots of pictures of Stephen on the mantel. There is also one of his mom holding his baby brother and a few pictures of his cousins. Whenever I take a roll of pictures I get doubles, so his mother can have some. She shares baby pictures of him with me.

The first picture on the mantel of Annie is one with her mother.

Mary
(the Author)

Sometimes I substitute in the Pulmonary Rehabilitation Clinic, when another nurse is out sick. I was working there one day, chatting with a particularly lovely patient while she walked on a treadmill. She was telling me how awful her last hospitalization had been.

"What happened?" I asked, expecting to hear how short of breath she had been or how many tries is took to get her IV in.

"My daughter and her family drove up from Pennsylvania to see me. They stopped in Rite-Aid before they even came to the hospital. The four-year-old started running around the store and his dad grabbed him and gave him a little spank on the bottom. By the time they paid for their things and went out to the car, the police were there. Somebody had called in that they were abusing their son."

So it really does happen, I thought, but I just encouraged her to go on with her story.

"They barely got out of the state with their kids and they're not coming back."

"So you'll have to go visit them," I said, knowing full well she would never see her grandchildren again. Her emphysema was much too advanced for her to travel.

CHAPTER 28

✦ ✦ ✦

Like Enron

When I took foster parent training I was told I would learn a lot about myself by taking in these kids. And I did. But I also learned more than I ever expected to about the system. With each new child another assumption was turned on its head.

With Marie I learned that kids' lives can get worse instead of better by being taken into foster care. And while the chaos of the biological family is blamed on the parents, any abuse in the foster home is blamed on the child. So the suffering of that child, the confusion, the loneliness, the longing for real family connections, is completely irrelevant.

From Tina I learned that some people in the system derive satisfaction "sticking it to" the birth parents. They enjoy their perceived superiority. It reminded me of the time we had a patient in the ICU because he had been shot committing a particularly heinous crime. We nurses had to admit it was freeing to feel no obligation to sympathize or comfort him as we did with other patients. It was just plain fun to hear him complain of pain and be able to answer with a smile, "Tough shit." Some DHS workers feel the same way about parents who have been labeled "bad." Tina's worker did. And she expected me to join right it. It is the culture of the organization.

When instead, I proved that Tina's behavior had an organic cause and was not the result of abuse…well, that wasn't important. She was in the system and going to stay there. No one went back to the parents and said, "We've made a mistake. You can have her back, but you'll

199

need help. What can we do?" I learned DHS means never having to say you're sorry.

In Brian's case the parent really was the villain and it was good to be reminded that it does happen. The intervention of the system is the only reason Brian will ever see adulthood. But, even with that, and the emotional response he elicited in all of us, Brian's individual needs were not important. His mother's Boston lawyer spoke louder than he did. I learned that while child abuse crosses socio-economic lines, the response to it does not.

Working in the emergency room has reinforced this. I have watched poorer parents be reported for having allowed their children to get a sunburn or for minor wounds that "might" have been inflicted or "could" have been inflicted by an adult. It makes me want to warn poor people never to seek medical care for their children. They have no idea that they walk in the door with the first and second strike against them already.

By the time I got Amy Lynn I already knew that the system forgot about the kids as soon as they had them placed and spent it's energy working against the parents. I knew decisions were made by front line workers who had minimal supervision and would be rubber-stamped by the judge more often than not. I didn't know before then that a mother could be put in a Sophie's Choice-like predicament forced to choose which children she wanted to keep and which ones she would be willing to give up. But it didn't surprise me.

I had very little sympathy for front workers by then, but I was willing to admit that they were over worked, that time constraints played a roll in their seeming indifference to the children in care. Then I found out that they really could find the time if they wanted to. If they decided to build a case against someone, this time me, they found the time.

I used to think the ideal foster parent was one who cared about the kids. By Amy Lynn I knew the ideal foster parent was one with the worker could have an unspoken agreement. You stay out of my life and I'll stay out of yours. I wasn't one of those. They needed to get rid of me. Or at the very least, show me who is boss.

I felt some of what the birth families must feel. I emphasize some, because I was not and never could be threatened with losing my biological children. They were already grown and gone. To go through that has to be the worst pain, the most frightening and helpless feeling in the whole world. If I project myself back to when I was a young mother, and imagine what it would have been like to be threatened with losing my children because I slipped up, well...it is unimaginable. Is it worse to have a child snatched off the lawn by a stranger in a van, never to be seen again? I'm not sure it is. It is barely any different.

Taking Michael showed me that there is hope. There are others within the system who have managed to maintain their humanity. His worker, Judith, is a ray of sunshine even on her worst days because she is so good at heart.

We have joked about winning the lottery and starting a private agency called Reunifications R Us. Her idea. The sad thing is, even with Judith and with other wonderful people on Michael's team, reunification isn't going to happen for him. Because, while her supervisor would not question a decision that put more distance between him and his family, and a judge would have no problem signing off on that, a lot of bells and whistles would go off if she suggested moving the opposite direction, toward sending him home. It was tough enough to reinstate visits with his mother.

The question that would be asked is how a child who is so damaged by six years in foster care that he needs a treatment level foster home possibly succeed with the same mother he was taken away from, who apparently couldn't handle him before he was damaged?

Treatment level kids never go home. They don't go to kinship placements and they don't go back to the reservation if they are Native Americans. Even though other states report that behaviors that led to the designation "treatment level" often go away once kids are back with their families, Maine isn't taking any chances. "Err on the side of the child" is their motto. If Judith were to suggest otherwise, her competence would be questioned.

Even after ten foster children, five long term and five short term or respite, a case could still be made for coincidence. Maybe I just happened to run into the worst workers in the state. Maybe I caught them all on a bad day. Maybe I could have handled some things better myself. So maybe the whole system shouldn't be judged on my experiences.

Then Logan Marr died.

The foster care system in Maine was the topic of conversation everywhere I went. From work to the grocery store line, everyone was talking about it and everyone had a story to tell. And they weren't telling third hand stories with the details blurred. They were personal. My learning curve went through the roof.

When the State Legislative hearings to investigate DHS began, my education continued. There seemed to be no end to the horror stories, each sadder than the one before.

A child really was taken because the mother refused to say "I love you" before the child left for school in the morning (after the child knocked over an entire china cabinet and broke everything in it). I read the court papers myself. I had learned in my mandatory class on reporting abuse that, refusing to say, "I love you," is emotional abuse. I just couldn't believe anyone really acted on it.

Another child, a fourteen-year-old boy, was taken when his father slapped him after catching him peeking through a keyhole at his sister changing clothes. The mother was told she could have her child back only if she got a divorce. According to my class on reporting abuse, a slap in the face, like a swat on the bottom, constitutes "immediate jeopardy." I barely know anyone who didn't spank their children at least once, when they went through the "running in traffic" phase, and slap them at least once when they tried swearing at parents for the first time. We share the stories at work and when we go out for coffee, never considering the possibility that we could be overheard and reported for child abuse. I guess on some level, we know we're safe. We have jobs, middle-class incomes and insurance. No one is watching us.

I could go on and on. But the bottom line is that I learned my kid's stories are not unusual. They aren't even shocking anymore after all the others I've heard that are more so.

The biggest shock of all came when the committees to investigate DHS released their findings and recommendations. They were disappointingly weak.

The same people I had watched turn beet red with anger said, in essence, "DHS, you should do better."

The same lawmakers who had wiped tears from their eyes during the public hearings said, "Maybe we shouldn't be fourth on the list of states when it comes to percentage of children in foster care. Maybe we should aim to be a little bit further down the list." They are going to check in once a year to see how the state is doing.

Can't you just hear the directive out of the administrative offices?

"Quick! We've got to send 200 kids back home to get the numbers down before the oversight committee gets here. Each office has to re-unify 10 families. Don't worry about which families, just do it. They'll be back in a few months anyway. We're pulling all supports and elimi-nating transition time, so the parents will fail. We'll have them back in no time and then we'll have a few horror stories of our own to tell."

Unfortunately, that is not just the product of my cynical mind. It is already happening. By now, others in the system who want something made public, but are afraid to speak out come to me. Good social work-ers and foster parents are having their hearts ripped out watching the wrong children go home to almost certain disaster. But the numbers will be fixed. That's all that matters to get us through this "foster care crisis." The children themselves remain irrelevant.

I guess if I had to sum up all that I have learned it is that the Child Welfare business is just that...a business. Children are the product. Children keep the business running and everyone employed. Child Welfare is a business just like Wal-Mart, like drug companies, like the tobacco industry, like Enron.

The only difference is that in Child Welfare is protected by confi-dentiality laws and immunity from prosecution. Imagine if the same could be said of other businesses.

CHAPTER 29

✦　✦　✦

If I Ruled the World

When I first began speaking out about the problems in the foster care system, I was frequently asked, "How can it be fixed?" I would answer, "It needs to be torn down and rebuilt from the vision on up." It was not a bad answer, because I have since learned that "vision" is part of the problem, but my answer reflected primarily that I didn't have answer.

Knowing something is wrong and knowing how to change an entire system are two different things. I compare it to the health care system. It is one thing to know when your medical care has been substandard. It is another to have a plan to change the entire system. It takes the right educational background as well as creativity and common sense.

Some people have that. I have met some of them in the past year, since the hearings to investigate DHS began. Thanks to them, I now have a better answer for the question how would I fix the system. But I don't want to steal their ideas. I want to give credit where credit is due.

The person who has educated me the most is Richard Wexler. He is the Executive Director of a non-profit organization called National Coalition for Child Protective Reform. Their website www.nccpr.org gives a nice summary of things that could be done differently to keep more children with their birth families. The site also gives examples of places in the country that have already implemented the changes and what they have seen in the way of results.

I will summarize even further what is on this website, adding my "two cents."

The first thing on his list of successful alternatives to taking children from their parents is, "Do nothing." When parents are innocent, apologize, shut the door and go away. I read that and thought, by today's definition of child abuse, no parent is innocent. It is that definition that has to be changed. I believe we have confused child abuse with parenting we don't agree with, when we have swats on the bottom and time-outs over 10 minutes on the list. I always remember a Donahue Show where he said, "Let's face it. Nobody believes in spanking, but everybody does it." It is that kind or realism that needs to be brought into play here.

The second thing on Mr. Wexler's list is, "Offer real concrete help." That makes me think of Stephen's mother. She needed a place to live and some financial help when she called DHS six years ago. She was in over her head with three children by the time she was eighteen and an absentee husband. A social worker came out to her apartment and promised her that help if she would just sign on the dotted line. The children would be kept together in foster care and she would have them back with her in a new apartment in six weeks…if she would just sign. She did.

Think how much money could have been saved if they had kept their promise to her. Stephen and his brother are both now treatment level, members of the $100,000 a year club.

Number three is, "Implement 'Intensive Family Preservation.'" There are many ways of doing family preservation and a variety of such programs around the country. Some are listed on the NCCPR website. I read in a women's magazine about one program where an entire small town was built up for "at risk" families. Parents could live there for two years, while getting an education at a local college. Housing and babysitting are paid for. Classes on parenting are mandatory. Families are closely supervised and helped when there is a problem, not penalized whenever possible. That is just one example. There are many more out there if the mission really is to keep families together.

The last thing on the list is, "Change financial incentives." That part is critical. Every step of the way money is involved. Everyone is paid; most are paid better if the children are worse off. The state gets federal money for every child in care, more if the child is deemed treatment level. Private agencies are paid for each day the child is in care. Money stops for everyone if the child goes home. Other states have found ways to set the system up so there is reward either way, to be sure decisions are made independent of personal financial gain.

One such state is Colorado, specifically El Paso County. That department is run by a man named David Berns, who was the first to give me concrete examples of what I meant when I said the system needed to be changed "from the vision on up." He successfully changed the vision in his part of the world and was able to keep families together and children safe at the same time.

First, he changed their mission from rescuing children from child abuse to preventing child abuse by attacking its two leading causes, poverty and domestic violence.

Then he changed child abuse investigations from "incident-focused," to "issue-focused." Incidents require someone to blame. Issues are problems that require solutions.

He also developed something called the "family wrap around." When a family is determined to be at risk, a five-member team descends on them to help solve their problems. One member of each team is an individual who was helped by the system themselves, someone whose family was in trouble, but is no longer.

Last, or should I say the last thing I remember, because nothing is so simple as to be accurately summarized in a few pages, he changed the thinking about money. Expenses to keep families together are always compared to the expense of a child in treatment level foster care. Helping families while keeping the children at home may cost the state some money, but treatment level foster care costs a whole lot more and has a worse outcome.

So now I have a better answer to the question, how would I fix the system. But I still don't want to do it myself. I want Judith to get the job!

UPDATES

✦ ✦ ✦

I ran into one of Tina's social workers one afternoon at L. L. Bean. I was shopping with a purchase order from DHS, so she was able to identify me as a foster parent while waiting in line behind me. We had never met before, but had spoken on the phone when Lillian had been unavailable. I asked her if she knew how Tina was doing. She said she thought she was still in a juvenile correction center in Northern Maine.

She added, "Did you believe her parents? That poor child never had a chance."

"It wasn't their fault she had behavior problems," I said. "She had a syndrome that led to chemical deposits on the brain. Behavior problems are part of the syndrome."

She didn't ask what the syndrome was. She didn't express dismay at what was apparently new information. She just continued on the subject of her awful parents. "They may not have caused her problems, but they sure didn't help."

✦ ✦ ✦

I got an email from Brian, soon after my editorial was in the Lewiston paper. He was living just 20 miles away. While it was true his mother was acquitted of all charges, he was not returned to her. Nor had he stayed with his uncle. He had been moved to live with an aunt after they had difficulty dealing with his laziness and lying. They aunt had the same problems and he had been moved to live with his stepfather's parents.

So he was in his fourth placement. He told me that he had asked if he could come back to live with me and was told I had said I wouldn't take him back. He thanked me for warning him that they would do that.

On the day he left I'd said, "Some day you're going to ask if you can call me, or come see me and they will tell you that I don't want to hear from you again, that I have moved on. Don't believe it. They say that to everyone. You are always welcome.

He wanted to come and visit, but I said I had to get his grandparents' permission. I called them and got more than that. I got an earful about what DHS had put them through and what DHS had told them about me. They had warned the grandparents not to let him see me because I had provided drugs and alcohol for him when he lived with me! Fortunately, they didn't believe it and we have had many nice visits with Brian since.

Unfortunately, his grandparents couldn't handle his behavior any better that his other relatives could, so he is now in a group home, and he is not allowed to call me.

A few months ago I got a call from Marie for the first time in two years. She was living with her boyfriend, about to graduate from high school, and she was "clean and sober." She wanted me to know that. She said the reason we had so many problems at the end was her drug use.

She started using drugs, pot initially, with her DHS worker on health and well-being checks. That news stunned me. I wanted to go find that worker myself and wring her neck. Marie begged me not to get her worker in trouble.

I encouraged her to go back to the lawyer, Caroline Gardiner, whom she had been seeing when she lived with me. She took the phone number.

When we got off the phone I realized she might have called a few days before her graduation for a reason. Maybe no one was going to be there to represent her family and she wanted me to go. So I did. But her family was there. I ran into them on the way into the building.

I left without seeing Marie.

It was about this time I learned that Amy Lynn's mother agreed to give her up for adoption, in exchange for getting her younger children back. I looked for her picture on the A Family for Me website but I didn't find it. That usually means she was adopted by someone who already was acquainted with her. Snooping got me as far as finding out that it was not her foster mother. It may well have been her counselor.

On June 25, 2002, Sally Schofield was convicted of manslaughter in the suffocation death of Logan Marr.

✦ ✦ ✦

Below are some of the things I have said or written during this year of the "Foster Care Crisis:"

Statement Made at the Investigative Hearing for the Health and Human Services Committee, September 2001

My name is Mary Callahan. I am a critical care nurse and the author of a book on raising a handicapped child. I'm also a foster parent. I went into foster parenting 6 years ago with my own bias. Only then, I didn't consider it a bias. To me, it was just knowledge of some basic facts. For example:

1. I assumed the children I would be caring for had been terribly hurt by their own parents, and had nowhere else to go.

2. I assumed I would meet some great people doing the work, people like me who wanted to give these kids a better chance at life.

Now, six years later, I have a new bias, but this time it is based on my own experiences.

First of all, many of the foster kids I've had were taken from their parents for some pretty minor reasons. In this committee's first meeting someone made a comment about DHS workers building a case based on rumor and innuendo. Someone else responded that anyone who did that ought to be fired. I can tell you from my experience that rumor and innuendo play a huge role. The child won't be taken based on it, but the family will be watched because of it until there is a "Gotcha" moment and then the child will be taken. The "Gotcha" moment for my kids have been as minor as one episode of discipline with a belt, or "rough handling" on the way to the car when the child was being suspended from school.

I've been in the trainings where we foster parents are taught to spot and report "Gotcha " moments, only in the classroom it isn't called that. It is called child abuse. In a recent class I was told the following was reportable child abuse:

- A time-out longer than 10 minutes,
- A parent refusing to hug a child who was asking for hug,
- A parent grabbing a misbehaving child by the arm and pulling him close to have words with him,
- A child being swatted on the bottom. This one, we were told, is abuse because "the buttocks are the most tender part of the body." This isn't even accurate information. The highest concentration of pain nerves is around the sense organs, like the eyes or the finger-tips.

By these standards, I suspect many among us would be considered child abusers. I know I would.

I have only had one child whose mistreatment by a parent even required medical attention. That child was nearly killed by his mother. He was in ICU at MMC just weeks before he came to me. He is also the only child I've ever had to be returned to his family. Of course, his family had money and that made all the difference.

As far as the great people I would meet...I've met a few. But I've also met some horrible people and some of them were foster parents.

The first child I had, the one who was taken from her family after one episode of discipline with a belt, spent six years with a foster mother who called her a slut, made her run up and down the driveway while the rest of the family ate, confined her to a completely barren bedroom for so many hours a day that she learned to relieve herself in a cup and pour it out the window. When a social worker was coming over, her foster mother warned her if she blew this placement she would end up in a trailer home with 20 other kids picking through the garbage for food.

Recently I was discussing this case with a social worker friend of mine. She was arguing that I base my opinions too much on this and a few other bad experiences. She told me she had kids in some wonderful foster homes. She started telling me about one in particular that she thought was great. But as she told it, her voice started to trail off. Then she admitted there was one problem in that home. One rule she was trying to get changed. It seemed the family had a backyard swimming pool. But it was off limits to foster kids. Only biological kids were allowed to swim. I think she was right that this is a more typical foster home than the example I gave. It looks good at first glance, but dig a little deeper, and you may find the child is being hurt in his real "most tender part," his sense of self-worth.

As far as the DHS workers I've dealt with…I have a great one now. But I've also had a DHS worker leave a message on my answering machine calling me a liar. Another told me not to call her again, after the first time I called. It didn't stop me. To be honest, I couldn't believe she meant it. I continued to call when there was something I thought she needed to know about the child. Finally, in exasperation, she told me, "You are just the caretaker. Your job is to feed him and drive him where he needs to go. Leave the thinking to the professionals."

That's when I figured out the obvious, what was staring me in the face all along. I drive DHS workers crazy because I keep calling about the child. And it's not about the child any more. It's about a power struggle between the workers and the bio-parents. By the time the child comes to me, he is completely irrelevant.

So…this is my new bias. We're taking children from places that are not that bad, putting them in places that are not that good, and leaving out of the equation completely the powerful bond that exists between parent and child, that is like a magnet, that just keeps pulling no matter what the distance between.

Last spring I took my 11-year-old foster son to Disneyworld. He hasn't seen his mother in over a year. He hasn't lived with her since he was four. And yet all he could say was, "I can't wait till I'm a grown-up and I can bring my mom back here."

Lastly, if there is one thing I would like to accomplish in my five minutes, it is to have you all stop and think when you use phrases like "protecting the children" and "child safety." What exactly do you mean by that? If you mean putting them in foster care, you may just be reflecting your own bias, but not reflecting the hard, cold truth.

Editorial I Had in
The Lewiston Sun Journal, July 2001

Although I knew DHS workers can act in bad faith, I was never a target until I moved to Lisbon. A year ago I decided to sell my house in

Portland and move to Lisbon. As a critical care nurse, I could work anywhere, but as a foster parent, I wanted more space.

I found the perfect spot. The house was a simple ranch with a big finished basement playroom. The yard was shaded, fenced and already furnished with a swing set, playhouse and tree fort. The foster child who spent the summer looking at houses with me kept saying, "This place is kid heaven." We made the move.

Six months later I was telling my lawyer that story. "You made a mistake moving here," she said. "Now you'll have to deal with Lewiston Department of Human Services." I had a lawyer because of Lewiston DHS.

I don't blame Amy, the child I had been accused of abusing. She was just a normal kid with a flare for the dramatic. She said outrageous things about everyone, but was the first to admit when she'd made it up. "I've been lying my whole life," she'd say. "I'm trying to stop."

We were working on that and making progress. I was reporting each incident to DHS, usually by voice mail. I rarely got a call back, except from the secretary who would call every week to tell me what time Amy's ride would be coming to take her to see her mother.

That information was often wrong. Once I was told the ride was coming at 9 A.M. when the arrangements were actually made for 4 P.M. Once the driver was given the wrong address and no one showed up.

In frustration I called Amy's guardian *ad litem* and complained. He was shocked to learn that the DHS wor ker had never even met Amy or visited our home. He rectified that situation.

Later an abuse charge was filed against me in what I believe was retaliation for my complaint.

I didn't learn about it for weeks. Amy was still with me and I hadn't been told there was a problem. I insisted they either drop the charge or take the child and they chose the latter. Amy left me a note saying I was "the gret fostemom."

We both cried.

When I finally had the charges read to me on the phone, I had to laugh. It was just typical Amy stuff. Anyone who knew her would have recognized that. The charge was eventually ruled "unsubstantiated," but Amy was gone and I will never work with Lewiston DHS again.

This is not to say that Lewiston is the worst or that this was the first time I had known a DHS worker to act in bad faith. This was just the first time I was the target. Usually, it's the biological family.

It was a Biddeford DHS worker who once told me she was setting a mother up to lose her child, little Tina, who was in my home. Knowing the child was originally take for some pretty flimsy reasons, I asked why she would do that.

"I've been in this town a long time," she told me. "I know this family and they are scum."

When the mother did fail to get to every meeting or class, keep a full time job and take care of her four remaining children, the worker called me to gloat.

"She was just here, crying in her beer. Must be nice to let the state raise your kids. That's what I wanted to say."

It was also a Biddeford worker who admitted to me that another child in my care, Marie, should have gone home years before.

"Her dad didn't do much for his own case. He kept coming into the office all loud and blustery, threatening to sue. The worker before me was determined not to let him win. So he blew things out of proportion to the judge. He was eventually fired for that sort of thing, but it was too late to send Marie home."

In the meantime Marie had spent years in abusive foster homes. In the first she was molested. In the second, she was starved, belittled and confined in her room for so long that she had to pee in a cup and dump it out the window. When I got her, she was malnourished and reading four years below grade level. But it wasn't about Marie anymore. It was a power struggle between adults, and, good news! We won!

Eventually I got to know both of these girls' parents. I liked them. I didn't think they were scum. As a matter of fact, I was struck by how alike we were, not how different.

I was so upset by Marie's story that I went up to the state legislature to speak to the Health and Human Services Committee twice. But I couldn't get on the docket. I did buttonhole one lawmaker in the hallway, though, and I started to tell him the story. He stopped me five minutes into it.

"We've got a hundred stories just like it," he said. "There is nothing new here."

That was three years ago and this is several foster kids later. I realize now he was right. Marie's story is pretty typical for this system.

So I knew, before I moved north, that DHS has an Us-Against-Them mentality that destroys families. What I learned from Lewiston is what it feels like to be Them. And I learned that I like Them more than I like Us.

Statement at the Press Conference on the Anniversary of the Death of Logan Marr

My name is Mary Callahan. I am a critical care nurse as well as a foster parent. The death of Logan Marr, one year ago today, did not open my eyes to the problems in the foster care system in Maine. It may have loosened my tongue, but my eyes were already wide open. They were opened by the kids who have spent time in my home, the foster kids I have had over the past seven years.

I take primarily older kids, who have been in the system for a while. Nine is the youngest I've had, so they have all been very capable of telling their own story. As it turns out, I'm a pretty good listener. And this is what the kids have told me.

In short, they feel that DHS took them from chaos and put them in hell. We've all heard the term "foster hell." It is used so often in stories about kids in foster care. It's like a shorthand and we all nod like we know what it means, but my kids gave me concrete examples of what it means. It means bouncing from home to home, being molested in one, beaten in the next and humiliated in the one after that. It means finding a pretty good placement only to have it end suddenly with no explanations or good-byes.

Foster hell is spending a year in a group home being intimidated by much older kids, then moving to a foster home deep in the woods where you are expected to spend your days memorizing Bible passages and are threatened with eternal damnation if you don't. Foster hell is being put on medications when you begin to assert yourself, chemical inducers of good behavior that buy time in the placement, but make kids feel like zombies. When eventually they refuse to take the meds, and teenage rebellion rears it's head, and no foster home wants them anymore, the kids begin the inevitable "shelter shuffle," that is so often the last chapter of a life in foster hell.

214

The kids talk about life before foster care too. They talk about hard times, moving from apartment to apartment. They talk about being left alone too much and moms that are sad a lot. But they talk with love about relatives, especially moms. They wish their moms had it easier and could have kept them.

I've only had two kids who didn't want to go back home. And one eventually realized that her bitterness towards her parents began when they told her on a supervised visit that they thought she should stay in foster care. She didn't realize they were forced by DHS to say that under threat of losing all visitation.

When kids first started telling me their stories, I didn't want to believe it. I wanted to think they were exaggerations. So I would check details with their DHS workers hoping for some explanation that would make it make sense. But I never got that. The kids were telling the truth. Sometimes I got responses like, "The child brought a lot of that on herself," which I thought was a cop out. But usually I got, "Let's just be happy she has a good foster home now. Let's focus on the positive." That has a familiar ring to it, doesn't it? I think we all know a little girl who was told, "Let's talk about happier things," when she complained about mistreatment by her foster mother. This is a specific form of denial.

Richard Wexler talks about DHS being in denial. As a critical care nurse, I am very familiar with denial. When patients or family members get bad news, denial buys them time to let the painful truth sink in.

But there are two kinds of denial. There is denial of the event and there is denial of the significance of the event. The second one is actually more common because it is easier to hang on to.

That's when the patient stops saying of his cancer diagnosis, "I don't believe it," and starts saying, "It's no big deal." It's when the family stops saying, "No, it can't be," when someone dies, and starts methodically planning a funeral. Both kinds buy time. Both avoid a painful truth.

I find DHS workers to be in denial of the significance of the information they have. They know a child was molested in one foster home and starved in another, but they rationalize by blaming the child or saying the biological family wasn't so great either. They refuse to look at the simple facts. Worse things happened to the child after he came into foster care than happened before. The child's life got worse, not better. The child has gone from chaos to hell. And this is very significant. If our purpose is to protect children, we're doing it wrong.

You have to wonder how this could happen, and to so many kids, but I attended a training last year that made it clearer. The training was on reporting child abuse and the list of reportable offenses shocked me. A time-out of longer than ten minutes is child abuse. Refusing to say, "I love you" is child abuse. A swat on the bottom is child abuse and that one, our trainer told us, "could be considered immediate jeopardy under some circumstances," meaning the child could be taken immediately. Under what circumstances is a swat on the bottom immediate jeopardy?

To most people this sounds completely absurd. Who would report someone for swatting a child on the bottom? What parent hasn't done it themselves?

But I actually had a hospitalized patient tell me that her grandchildren couldn't visit her anymore, because the last time they drove up from Pennsylvania for a visit, someone called the police when the four year old got a swat on the bottom in Rite-Aid. As the grandma put it to me, "They barely made it out of the state with their kids and they aren't coming back."

We have lowered the bar on what is considered child abuse to the point where Maine has the 4th highest percentage of its children in foster care in the country. Now we need so many foster homes for all those kids that we are practically begging on the street corners. There are ads on TV and booths in the mall. It seems we're ready to take anyone who is willing to take the check. Last year I had a driver, hired by DHS, who picked up my foster child and drove her to visit her mother ever Saturday. Chatting with the driver one day I learned that she herself had grandchildren in foster care and had been denied a kinship placement and her grandchildren were being put up for adoption. So DHS is actually hiring people to care for other people's kids, who they have rejected to care for their own. This isn't just illogical. It is sick. And DHS is in denial.

Apparently, so are the committees who have been investigating the foster care system in Maine since Logan Marr's death. As a concerned foster parent and a citizen of Maine, I attended almost every meeting, listened to and read most of the testimony. And I was very impressed at

216

how quickly the committees got to her heart of the matter by listening both to national experts and Mainers with stories to tell. I was optimistic that things were going to change. But when I read the final reports, I felt like the committee members and I had been at two different meetings.

I was particularly stunned when I read that they saw "no hard evidence" of children being removed unnecessarily. I heard plenty of it. I presented plenty of it in my testimony at the public hearings. Besides that, I was on "Mainewatch" and quoted in *The Portland Press Herald*. I have written letters to the editors of most major newspapers in this state, and even had an editorial of my own in the *Lewiston Sun Journal*. I feel like the kid in the back of the classroom waving her hand madly while the teacher says, "So if there are no more questions, we'll move on." I have communicated my kids' stories in ever way I could think of and yet no one, not one committee member, not one DHS official has ever called me and said, "Tell me more. We need to know what is really going on."

Denial is a comfortable place to be. Especially compared to accepting the fact that one has cancer or that one's agency has a disease just as serious.

Lastly, we are here today because it is a specific date, the anniversary of the death of Logan Marr. But I would like to talk for a moment about a different date, one that affected all of us very deeply, and at least for a time, made us all look at what is really important in life. That date is, of course, September 11. I happened to be at a team meeting that morning for my foster son. When the two social workers and I learned what was going on in New York City and Washington D. C. we stopped what we were doing and just stared at the TV like the rest of the country. When it sank in, we all looked each other and had the same thought. We needed to get my foster son from school and let him call his mother.

My DHS worker, who I have to say is a rare gem, went back to her office to call the other children on her caseload to give them the same opportunity to talk to their biological families.

For that brief moment our vision was clear. No one was in denial. We knew what was important and that is the love of family.

If only we could remember that every day. I'd like to aim, not just for never having another Logan Marr, but for never having another Marie or Tina or Anthony or Graham or Annie. Those are just a few of the kids who have been in my care and who I am speaking for today.

Editorial I Had in
The Portland Press Herald, April 2002

As a foster parent for the past seven years, I have been subjected to the Us-Against-Them, I-Win-You-Lose mentality of DHS workers many times.

Other foster parents know exactly what I am talking about. For the uninitiated, it means you either agree with your caseworker or you will be punished.

It took me years to ask these questions: If they treat foster parents this badly, how must they treat biological parents? And how many children have been caught in the crossfire, sent to unsafe foster homes just to show their parents who is boss? At least two of the foster children who have spent time in my home fit that description.

Earlier this month, I believe I witnessed the genesis of the DHS mindset.

DHS Commissioner Kevin Concannon showed up unannounced at a seminar for foster and adoptive parents that I attended. He got up in front of the group and used his time, not to talk about helping the families and children of Maine, but to gloat over his perceived win in his battle against his critics in the media, namely Richard Wexler of the National Coalition for Child Protective Reform.

He even threw in a personal insult for Wexler when he said that the man made a better impression in print than he did in person.

Concannon went on to say that the investigation of DHS done by the two committees of the state legislature found only minor issues to work on and he felt, all in all, he had proved his critics wrong. (In fact, one of the committees did recommend significant changes in DHS procedures.)

He went on to list all of his accomplishments like a lower rate of teen pregnancy and improved prescription drug coverage as he does every time the name Logan Marr comes up. Does anyone think children in pain care about Concannon's other accomplishments? That's like saying the man who just had the wrong leg amputated should take solace in the fact that the patient in the next bed had the correct operation. One has nothing to do with the other. One does not negate the other.

It was particularly disheartening listening to him after spending the morning in a lecture by David Berns, the director of human services in El Paso County, Colorado.

Berns talked about reforms that led to a 25 to 30% decrease in kids in foster care and a 40% decrease in institutional placements, as well as a dramatic increase in kinship care and special needs adoptions.

He described a system in which 100% of adoptions are by family members or foster parents, where out of the last 900 adoptions, only one was later dissolved. All of this was done without jeopardizing the safety of children or straining the budget. As a matter of fact, Berns described the changes as "budget neutral."

What reforms could work this kind of miracle? Common sense, compassion and a philosophy that says if you eliminate poverty and domestic violence, children will automatically be safer, and with their own families.

Ah, compassion. There wasn't much of that in evidence when one of Concannon's workers took a bow when introduced as "The Terminator" on the second day of the conference because she had terminated parental rights 50 times in three years, apparently a record.

And to think just the day before we had learned that in other parts of the country a lower number of terminations is considered something to brag about.

What is it about Maine that sets us apart from the rest of the country when it comes to foster care?

There must be something. Every time DHS is confronted with the fact that Maine has a very high percentage of its children in foster care, they respond that there is a good reason for that, but you have to be from Maine to understand it. Outsiders like Richard Wexler don't get it.

What does that mean? Are they saying Mainers are less intelligent than citizens of other states? Meaner? Drunker? Crazier?

Personally I think what sets us apart can be said in two words: Kevin Concannon.

Kevin Concannon's Response in *The Portland Press Herald,* One Week Later

I spoke at the recent gathering of Maine foster and adoptive parents, something I have done each year since becoming commissioner of Department of Human Services.

A subsequent column in this paper distorted these remarks and made unfounded allegations about DHS caseworkers and personal and vitriolic attacks about my management of Child Protective Services in our state.

To respond I would like to use this space to identify recent improvements in the child welfare system that have taken place since the tragic death of Logan Marr last year.

The Legislature, through the work of the Health and Human Services and the Judicial Committees, held hearings this past session to allow input from all interested parties on suggestive reform.

Based upon these efforts, legislation was passed that will provide more protection for children and also provide more assistance to parents who, for various social, economic and personal reasons are having difficulty providing a secure environment for their children.

First, the Legislature changed the rules governing access to child custody proceedings. A new law will allow anyone with a significant relationship to a child, such as a grandparent, aunt, uncle, teacher or coach, to observe and participate in child custody hearings.

The law preserves the confidential nature of these hearings, while at the same time opening up the process to individuals whose input will provide the court with a more complete understanding of the child's circumstances. Funds have also been allocated to hire paralegals whose specific responsibility will be to assist parents in child custody hearings.

Second, based upon the efforts of the governor, the legislature, and DHS, several new initiatives for child services have been approved.

Recognizing that efforts should be made to increase care by relatives of children who, for their own safety, are removed from their biological parents, there will be additional screening and training that promotes kinship care of foster children.

Recognizing that more than half of the children who come into DHS care are from families where a parent is a substance abuser, and that many parents choose not to enroll in substance abuse services provided by DHS, there will be new programs to better encourage chemically dependent parents to make use of treatment services.

Third, the Legislature and DHS have agreed to safely reduce the number of children in custody by 5%. Experts testified that Maine's child welfare workers have caseloads much higher than the national average. Additional caseworkers, licensing staff and family support services will be hired and this will allow caseworkers to spend more time working with the families of children in DHS care.

I took the occasion at the foster families conference to mention several statistics that affect child welfare in Maine. They bear repeating here.

Maine has one of the best rates in the nation providing health insurance to low income children. We are fourth highest for providing food stamps to eligible families, the vast majority of these beneficiaries being children.

We are fifth highest in obtaining financial child support for custodial parents and in reducing teen pregnancy, a severe risk for later child abuse. We are one of only two states to support ongoing higher education for head of welfare families.

The author took exception to this, suggesting that these figures have nothing to do with child welfare. She is wrong. Poverty is the leading risk factor for later child abuse. DHS has worked diligently to implement humane, family friendly welfare reform. This is essential in the effort to reduce the numbers of children in custody.

The principal mission of this department has been and continues to be to support families in their care giving roles as much as possible. The new child welfare legislation, by opening court proceedings to interested parties, providing additional services to parents in need and giving caseworkers more time to work with families, will assist in doing that.

As we attempt to reduce the numbers of kids in care, however, we cannot ignore the awful fact that there is physical, mental and sexual abuse of Maine children.

It is DHS's statutory responsibility to identify those children and, when necessary, ask the courts to protect them.

Op Ed I Had in the
Bangor Daily News, June 24, 2002

Every time I see Christy Marr, the mother of dead foster child Logan Marr, on television, I feel like I know her. Yet I have never met her.

I guess she reminds me of so many other mothers I've met, birth mother of the foster kids I've had in my home. They all share that same haunted look.

I think Tim McGraw says it best in a country song when he describes a woman as having years of bad decisions written on her face.

The woman in the song is homeless, but she has her child "wrapped around her legs." Christy and the mothers I know are haunted because they don't. They made enough bad decisions to lose them to Department of Human Services.

What kind of bad decisions can cost a mother her children? Choice of men is a big one. If a woman chooses an abusive man, and the children witness the abuse, that's considered failure to protect, as well as emotional abuse. Choosing a bad baby-sitter can be failure to protect as well, if the baby-sitter does something to hurt the child.

Leaving the child without a baby-sitter is an example of neglect. Then there is medical neglect. As an emergency room nurse I've seen cases of that called in. Once a 4 year old was brought in with a bad sunburn. It was neglect because it was day three of the sunburn and the first time the mother sought help. Just being an alcoholic can cost you your children, though experts say alcoholism is a disease, not a life style choice.

The worst decision is to let life's stresses beat you down so far you take it out on your children, with hitting, refusing to say "I love you" and overly long time-outs (10 minutes is the limit). Those things all qualify as abuse not neglect.

What kind of woman makes these bad choices? Young, poor and single ones more than mature, educated and married ones. At least to look at the foster care rolls that appears to be true. Though I have to say I was 27, educated and married when I started my family and I made a lot of bad decisions. I made some of the same bad decisions I just mentioned (my son still has scars from the sunburn) yet no one threatened to take my children. We all have low points in our life, weak moments in parenting. That's all my bad decisions were. That's why DHS let me have a foster care license in spite of my failings.

But in the end, the women who really make the worst parents are the ones who had the worst parents. They may love their children and desperately want to do right by them, but they never learned how. Some never learned how to take care of themselves, let alone a child. So their children end up in the hands of the state. Hence, the haunted look. They failed to protect their children from the worst abuser of all, DHS.

Logan Marr was moved from foster home to foster home, back to Mom, then back in care again. She was choked in one foster home and killed in the next.

But the foster kids I've had in my home have suffered almost as much as Logan in our attempt to keep them safe from bad mothers. First they all have them emotional trauma of the removal itself. Kids who were removed because they witnessed domestic violence say the removal was far more painful.

Several of my foster kids had been molested in foster care. Others were beaten. One was threatened by his foster father who said he was going to come back and find him some day and blow his brains out. Another was starved, isolated and humiliated by a particularly sadistic foster mother.

Some of us work hard to provide good homes for our foster kids. But we become just another stop on the road to hell when they are moved with no warning and no explanation, just when they were beginning to get comfortable. It happens all the time.

In the end these kids suffer the worst kind of serial parenting. They have to learn a new set of rules every time they move to a new home. They are too stressed to learn anything at school. They have trouble making friends, and if they do, it is only with other damaged children.

Many eventually give up on following anyone's rules. They are going to make terrible citizens some day and terrible parents. As long as we, as a society, choose to remove children rather than help their parents do better, you can be sure those children will go on to produce the next generation of foster children. It is a cycle, but not a hopeless one. Just one we have allowed to become hopeless.

I pray no one else ever has to face what Christy Marr is facing. But I wouldn't bet on it.

ADDITIONAL READING

Books

Bernstein, Nina. *The Lost Children of Wilder: The Epic Struggle to Change Foster Care*. Pantheon, 2001.

Bush, Malcolm. *Families in Distress: Public, Private and Civic Responses*. University of California Press, 1988.

Jones, E. P. *Where is Home? Living Through Foster Care* Four Walls Eight Windows, 1990.

Pelton, Leroy. *For Reasons of Poverty: A Critical Analysis of the Public Child Welfare System in the United States*. Praeger, 1989.

Pelzer, David J. *A Child Called "It": One Child's Courage to Survive*. Health Communications, 1995.

Roberts, Dorothy. *Shattered Bonds: The Color of Child Welfare*. Basic Civitas Books, 2002.

Schorr, Lizbeth B. *Within Our Reach: Breaking the Cycle of Disadvantage*. Anchor Press/Doubleday, 1988.

Schorr, Lizbeth B. *Common Purpose: Strengthening Families and Neighborhoods to Rebuild America*. Anchor Press/Doubleday, 1997.

Toth, Jennifer. *Orphans of the Living: Stories of America's Children in Foster Care*. Touchstone Books 1998.

Wexler, Richard. *Wounded Innocents: The Real Victims of the War Against Child Abuse*. Prometheus Books, 1990.

Magazine Articles

Gordon, Akka. "Taking Liberties." *City Limits*. December, 2000. A former caseworker for the child protection agency in New York City describes how the agency really works.

Katz, Alyssa. "Impaired Judgment." *City Limits*. February, 1999.

Nauer, Kim. "Guilty Until Proven Innocent." *City Limits*. November, 1994.

ACKNOWLEDGMENTS

✦ ✦ ✦

I would like to acknowledge all the help I have received along the way, first, in surviving being a foster parent, second, in confronting the problems of the foster care system, and third, in writing this book.

The kids themselves are the main reason I have survived. I thank them for letting me share in their lives and for brightening mine. Professionals who have kept my head above water include Judith, Carolee, Laurel, Rusty, and Carl.

Many have supported my move to go public with my experience as a foster parent. Most would prefer not being named, as DHS retaliation is legend. A few who won't mind and deserve a lot of credit are Richard Wexler, Jim LaBrecque, Chris L'Hommidieu, Stavros Mendros, and Terrilyn Simpson. Co-workers at St. Mary's Emergency Room and Southern Maine Medical Center's Cardiopulmonary Rehab Department renewed my energy whenever it was flagging.

Friends who kindly agreed to read the manuscript at its various stages and risk hurting my feelings with their criticism include Mary Cameron, Chris Brown, Deb Brown, and Nina Miller. Jesse Schweppe did the professional editing and became a friend in doing so.

Lastly, my birth children deserve a great deal of thanks. They made mothering so much fun, I wanted to do it again and again and again. Besides that, Tony changed me from a mere mother to a mother/crusader. And Renee changed a manuscript into a book with hard work, attention to detail, creativity, and enthusiasm.

Thanks everybody!

Give the Gift of

Memoirs of a Baby Stealer

to Your Friends and Colleagues

CHECK YOUR LEADING BOOKSTORE OR ORDER HERE

❑ **YES**, I want _____ copies of *Memoirs of a Baby Stealer* at $9.95 each, plus $4.00 shipping per book (Maine residents please add $.50 sales tax per book). Canadian orders must be accompanied by a postal money order in U.S. funds. Allow 15 days for delivery.

❑ **YES**, I am interested in having Mary Callahan speak or give a seminar to my company, association, school, or organization. Please send information.

My check or money order for $_____ is enclosed.

Please charge my: ❑ Visa   ❑ MasterCard

Name _____

Organization _____

Address _____

City/State/Zip _____

Phone_____ E-mail _____

Card # _____

Exp. Date_____ Signature _____

Please make your check payable and return to:

Pinewoods Press
PO Box 238 • Lisbon, ME 04250

Call your credit card order to: 917-553-6619
Fax: 207-353-7479 / Web site: www.babystealer.com

1/16 9 AM

margaret maccotte